The NEW F* WORD

The NEW F* WORD

THE ONLY BOOK ON EARTH THAT EXPOSES HOW TO BECOME *FUNDABLE

AND ACCESS HIGHLY-GUARDED, INEXPENSIVE LENDER MONEY

MERRILL CHANDLER

The New F* Word

THE ONLY BOOK ON EARTH THAT EXPOSES HOW TO BECOME *FUNDABLE, AND ACCESS HIGHLY-GUARDED, INEXPENSIVE LENDER MONEY

The Fundable Company
Salt Lake City, Utah

GetFundable.com
Info@GetFundable.com
www.GetFundable.com
801.438.9080

Ordering Information:
Special discounts are available on quantity purchases by corporations, associations, educational institutions, and others. For details, contact The Fundable Company above.

Printed in the United States of America
Second Edition

ISBN 978-1-5136-5723-3

Photography and cover design:
Michael Patwin and Lea Molina

Illustrations and editing:
Skigh Copier

Dedication

To all the past and present members of my team: Thank you for helping me turn into reality the theories that first started on that 8 x 10 wall so many years ago.

To Brad and Jessica: Thank you for your unfailing commitment to catch the fly balls of my mad scientist self and translate them into a message and form that can now be heard by millions.

To Steph and Laurie: Thank you for creating an environment of inspiration and deep support that has allowed me to chase down my dreams like a lion after a gazelle in the Serengeti.

To Sharon, Aaron, and Melissa: I continue to be amazed at how each of you navigate the journey of this life with power and resilience. To walk this unrelenting path with you is one of the greatest gifts of my life.

To all my students and clients: Thank you for believing in me and this process, and providing me the opportunity to prove over and over that *Fundability Optimization*™ can radically improve the lives of everyone it touches.

To all who have ever played the role of Chandler Handler: It is no small feat to clean up the proverbial china shop after my passing. Thank you for wrangling the stupidity and genius of my life.

To all of you: I am eternally grateful that you know me...and still choose to love me.

Author's Note

This book is not for sheep. Earl Nightingale said one of the greatest quotes about success that I've ever heard:

"Statistically, the majority is wrong most of the time.
If you want to be wrong most of the time, do what everybody else does."

This book is for the person that is willing to separate themselves from the "herd." And by doing so, they know it is their only chance at greatness!

Now having said that, let's get to it.

What is now known as *Fundability Optimization*™ was born in the Salt Lake County Jail in the Fall of 2001.

We'll come back to that.

For over a decade, I have implemented this revolutionary technology exclusively with high net-worth entrepreneurs, real estate investors, and business owners—most of whom I met while speaking at business and real estate investment conferences around the country.

For a long time, my partners, clients, and students have asked me to put into writing what I know about the financial principle I call *fundability.* I define fundability as the ability to be approved for funding via unsecured stated-income credit applications[1]— especially approvals using automatic underwriting systems (AUS).

While I have always wanted to share this wicked cool tech with a broader audience, taking the time to write this book required my *personal* attention. The tech is so specific and unique, I couldn't use a ghost-writer to do it for me.

---

[1] To reflect the new paradigm you are exploring and to be more accurate, I will refer to credit applications as funding requests and funding applications. You are looking for a Lender to give you access to cold hard cash (aka funding). The instrument the Lender uses is not important.

Consequently, this book represents the daunting task of *me* sitting down and focusing for endless hours to get it done.

So here it is.

And I am very proud of what you hold in your hands.

It contains the Principles of Fundability.

And for an introduction to a subject that is probably new to you, it is extremely comprehensive.

What I can promise is that you will learn many incredible—maybe even revolutionary—things to improve your fundability, both now and for the rest of your life.

But just like you can paint countless pictures with only a few paint colors, you will soon learn that you can use the numerous Fundability Principles you will find here to paint your unique and particular version of financial success.

And how you implement these Principles—individually and collectively—has a direct impact on your funding approvals.

Between you and me, I intend to blow your mind, disrupt your current beliefs, and even make you feel bad—in a good way.

This book is one of the many ways that I am committed to transforming the relationship between Borrowers and Lenders. By the end of this book, you will know FOR YOURSELF that successful borrowing is NOT based on the old beliefs about "good credit/bad credit" but is wholly and completely based on the NEW paradigm of FUNDABLE/NOT FUNDABLE. I *guarantee* (strong language, I know) that if you shift your focus to this new way of looking at funding, borrowing, and lending, your financial world (and life) will dramatically change—IN YOUR FAVOR.

Part of that dramatic change will be the realization that you have TOTAL power over your ability to get funding—and in turn, the power to shape your financial and personal destiny.

Disclaimers

1. I do not have access to FICO®2 or Lender underwriting software.

2. While I have had extensive meetings over the years with the score development teams, scientists, and executives at FICO®, they have not provided specific answers to EVERY question I have asked. But most of their answers *were* specific enough that they asked me to sign a Non-Disclosure Agreement.

3. Everything you will learn in this book is the culmination of 27 years of experience in analyzing and leveraging the approval patterns of innumerable Borrower Behavior profiles, FICO® scoring metrics, and Lender underwriting requirements.

4. I don't believe in "get rich quick" systems. I DO believe in dedicated work, creating value, building a professional enterprise, and empowering others. My educational offerings are designed to help you become personally and professionally fundable. My process requires dedication and discipline—just like any worthwhile professional development program.

5. Please don't engage in my process if you want to take *shortcuts* to get funding. I do not make any guarantees or promises about your ability to get a particular result with my education, strategies, or process. Any and all numbers, case studies, or results I refer to in my materials or presentations are used for illustration purposes ONLY and are NOT to be considered actual or implied results. Any results, and the time it takes to achieve said results, will vary based on your fundability, financial situation, and speed of strategy implementation.

---

2 FICO® stands for Fair Issac Company—the industry leader in predictive analytics. Its credit scoring software suite—FICO® Score™—is used by Lenders nation-wide to facilitate over 90% of all lending decisions in the United States.

Table of Contents

Introduction

I intend to bridge the gap that currently exists between Borrowers and Lenders.

I am committed to transforming the relationship between them from one of suspicion, distrust, and animosity to one of partnership, collaboration, and profitability.

To begin any reconciliation process, someone has to "go first." Someone has to see that the current situation is not working and CHOOSE to do something different.

That "someone" is me—and YOU.

The goal of this book is to reveal that there is a better way—a RIGHT way—to borrow money and work with Lenders. A way in which we can create everything WE want, and give Lenders exactly what THEY want as well.

This will happen as you discover how to become a "Professional" Borrower (more on this later).

But to change EVERYTHING, you must first change ONE THING.

YOU must change YOUR relationship with each of YOUR Lenders.

In these pages, you will learn a new frame of reference that will change how you think of Lenders and your relationship with them.

You will discover:

- *The insider secrets and strategies that will demonstrate to Lenders that you know how to create a prosperous and profitable relationship with them—in terms they understand*

- *How generous Lenders are when they feel there is little-to-no risk to lend to you, and how you can show them that lending to YOU is not only safe, but a huge win for THEM*

The Ugly Truth

The dysfunction between Borrowers and Lenders is all about trust— or lack of it. Neither party trusts the other, yet neither can prosper alone.

For good or ill, they need each other to succeed. It is the ultimate codependent relationship. But...

Lenders distrust Borrowers.

This situation has existed for centuries—and with good cause. Borrowing and lending is a messy business. This has resulted in Lenders experiencing a low-grade, dull, background fear that after all is said and done, Borrowers will lie, cheat, and steal from Lenders to get money.

Conversely, Borrowers distrust Lenders.

Borrowers have a low-grade, dull, background fear that after all is said and done, Lenders will financially pillage, plunder, and abuse Borrowers to make the most money they can from them.

And yet, since the beginning of time, Lenders have been willing to lend, and Borrowers have been willing to borrow, because each of them has believed it was worth the risk.

Since this book is about Borrowers "going first" and seeking to bridge the gap with Lenders, we must first understand Lender motivations and protection strategies. With this understanding, Borrowers can make choices and behave in a way that will create a trusting partnership with Lenders.

These choices will result in Borrowers having the funds and resources to fulfill their dreams. At the same time, these choices will demonstrate that Borrowers know how to honor and respect the resources they receive from Lenders.

The endgame here is a wildly prosperous partnership for both. The perfect win/win.

Lender Protection Strategies

There are three fundamental protection strategies that Lenders use to minimize their risk and uncertainty:

1. Frame Borrower/Lender Relationships in Absolute Terms

Borrowers currently think of their relationship with their Lenders in terms of *good* vs *bad*. This indoctrination is furthered by the common notion that a Borrower has either "good" credit or "bad" credit.

This misdirection keeps Borrowers in a fog of misinformation about what funding requests are actually based on. If you have "good" credit, you are never told why you were approved. And if you have "bad" credit, their solution is to tell you to "pay your bills on time."

So why all the mystery?

2. Predict the Future

The most important way Lenders can lower their risk with Borrowers is by being able to *predict* Borrower behaviors—and it's not as crazy an idea as you would think.

To do so, the Credit Bureaus must collect as much Borrower *performance data*[3] on as many Borrowers as possible.

Next, the performance data must be evaluated and measured by FICO® to determine Borrower behavior patterns that can be used to predict the likelihood of a behavior continuing into the future.

---

[3] This is the term Lenders use to describe how you act in your relationship with them and how you treat their funds.

Finally, with this predictive formula, automatic underwriting software can decide whether or not (and how much) to lend to a Borrower.

In these pages, you will discover how to intentionally trigger positive funding approvals by giving Lenders EXACTLY the measurable behavior they need to trust you with their funds.

Some skeptics may say that what you are learning here is a manipulation of the credit system...

That's like saying eating well, exercising regularly, and being a non-smoker is manipulating the health insurance system to get better rates.

You know that these behaviors are good for you, and the insurance system rewards you with lower rates for doing so.

It's the same with aligning your Borrower Behaviors with Lender funding criteria. Treating Lender funds with deference and respect is the right thing to do. It's a bonus that such behavior is rewarded.

3. Distract Borrowers from What is Being Measured

FICO® and Lenders have been very quiet about what they measure. Based on current results, they likely believe the only way to discover the "real" intentions and motivations of a Borrower is to measure their *unconscious* behaviors.

Therefore, to distract you from what they are REALLY measuring, Lenders give you something to else focus on. The perfect distraction turned out to be your "credit score."

To make matters worse, Borrowers have been led to believe they have ONLY ONE credit score.

This all-encompassing LIE results in Borrowers being left completely in the dark as to the truth of the matter.

For example, most Borrowers think that an 800+ credit score is fantastic—and they focus their efforts on achieving it. Sadly, I have met hundreds of Borrowers with 800+ scores who can't get a dime of funding to grow their businesses or reach their financial goals.

Why is that?

When you focus on your credit score, you completely limit your ability to get funding. It's like buying a car and focusing on the paint job when you should be looking at how well the engine runs.

An Amazing Opportunity

So far, it would appear that the protection strategies Lenders have been using are less-than-straightforward. I cannot disagree, but I take a different view of the whole thing. Remember, these are *protection* strategies they are using. They are trying to anticipate the very worst behavior from Borrowers.

This is GREAT news for Borrowers.

As you will find in this book, these protection strategies actually REVEAL what Lenders need *from you* to feel safe lending *to you*.

All the vast technology Lenders use—the algorithms, data mining, behavioral modeling, deep learning, AI machine learning, and predictive analytics—are strategies to protect themselves from loss.

But what if Lenders didn't have to protect themselves from you?

In these pages, you will learn how to stop stepping on the funding landmines that have limited your ability to get funding.

You will also discover that *the one thing* that will help you increase the number and amount of your funding approvals is to implement the strategies of *Fundability Optimization*™.

You will also learn what Lenders need to see to approve your funding requests *in less than 30 seconds*.

These "instant approvals" are the direct result of being *fundable*.

Take a moment to consider these questions:

- *What would it mean to you to know that what you learn here is the result of extensive meetings over several years with FICO® score development team members, and have been validated and proven by thousands of Borrowers just like you?*

- *What would it mean to you if you knew how to become fundable— even if your credit was less-than-perfect?*

- *How much money are you losing because you can't get approved for the very best interest rates and terms because you are not fundable?*

- *How much more opportunity would you have and how many more deals could you do if you were?*

- *How valuable would it be to discover the "real" process of funding approvals AND learn how to access the REAL credit scores Lenders actually use to approve your funding requests?*

- *What if you knew which type of accounts would add significant fundability to your Borrower Profile AND drastically increase the number and amount of your funding approvals?*

- *How would it change things for you if you knew how to get regular credit limit increases on both personal and business accounts without needing a credit inquiry, income verification, financial statements, or tax returns?*

The answers to these questions are deeply personal. And I promise, in these pages, you will find meaningful answers to these questions and so many more.

The Next Step

Until now, the concept of *fundability* has been reserved for the inner sanctums of FICO® and Lender underwriting strategists.

As you come to understand and adopt the Principles of Fundability, your entire life is going to change.

Why?

Because you cannot move from a position of funding *powerlessness* to a position of *total power* without something deep inside of you being transformed at the same time.

And that transformation will radiate from inside of you in the form of confidence, skill,  clarity, and peace of mind. In turn, your new level of confidence and skill will translate into more opportunities, more wisdom, and a higher quality of life.

Or at least that is what my students and clients tell me.

I have compared the relationship between Borrowers and Lenders to a game—*The Funding Game*. Specifically, I like to compare it to the game of basketball.

I use this analogy because it not only describes Borrower and Lender dynamics well, it also reveals that when we:

1) Learn the rules of how the Game is played...

2) Implement the strategies revealed in this book...

3) Practice just enough to gain a little mastery of these strategies...

4) We will no longer play like amateurs in a pick-up game at the local recreation center—we will play like Championship All-Stars.

And playing the Funding Game like a Pro changes EVERYTHING.

The more of us that learn how to play this Game like Pros, the more prosperity we will experience. Period.

To that end was this book written.

As of the printing of this 2nd edition, my team and I have helped our students and clients get over $103,000,000 in funding approvals using these *Fundability Optimization*™ strategies—while improving their standard of living and quality of life in the process.

Now it falls to you, dear reader, to make your own determination as to the funding possibilities available to you as you implement what you will learn in these pages. Like thousands before you, I urge you on this amazing and prosperous journey.

May each of us—Borrowers and Lenders—see the value of working together and playing on the same team.

We all win if we do.

Chapter 1

FICO World: The Break-Through That Changed It All

Beige...I think I'll paint the ceiling beige...

For my entire stay, that joke never got old because, like the unsatisfied housewife in the joke, I was laying on my back with nothing to do but look at the dull gray ceiling above me. But in my case, it was the ceiling of my 6' x 10' cell in the medium-security unit of the Salt Lake County Jail.

The severity of my charges required that I be on lockdown 18 hours per day with only my thoughts, a golf pencil, a pad of paper, and the random "cellie" for company.

But in truth, I wasn't alone...

There I was, over 10 years after the birth of *Fundability Optimization™*, when it happened.

For 10 years my team and I had been using my *Fundability Optimization™* tech to help Borrowers get the funding approvals that would save them thousands each year in interest and fees, allow them to qualify for the most inexpensive funding available, and change their lives for the better.

We had been using the tools that slowly made their way from the hallowed halls of FICO® to fine-tune our optimization tech to such a degree that we could, with increasing accuracy, predict when a client would be approved for the very best funding available.

We had weathered the financial collapse of 2008 and even helped our clients to avoid major financial disasters with well-informed preparation.

We were doing well.

Or so we thought. We discovered that even with all our success (and the confidence that went with it), we were still only playing "rookie" ball.

Then it happened...

We got called up to the Pros.

(Just like I am challenging you to learn how to play the Funding Game like a Pro, I had to accept that very challenge myself.)

An Amazing Discovery

In the Fall of 2015, Hannah[4], one of the members of my Executive Team, was doing some research on FICO® scoring models.

She discovered a little-known forum that would provide us a quantum leap in our knowledge of optimization AND our ability to make Borrowers fundable.

It was called FICO World...

We soon discovered that this gathering was the metaphorical Mount Olympus of the Funding Approval Gods. It was designed to be the most important gathering of the "who's who" in the world of lending and underwriting.

This conference was the place where Lenders, underwriters, and industry *"quants"* (quantitative analysts), would gather to learn what the FICO® Funding Approval Gods had been developing—and in the finance world, this meant measuring and predicting Borrower Behavior to better protect Lenders from loss.

This conclave occurred every 18 months and we were going to be a part of it. And as we learned later, we were the ONLY Borrower-facing organization in attendance!

When we applied to attend, FICO® staff vetted our website and social media profiles. We concluded that they wanted to know why

---

[4] Hannah Yandow was one of my Executive Team members who attended our first FICO World and was instrumental in helping me expand the influence of this technology. She was a huge contributor and inspiration to what Fundability Optimization™ has become today.

we were applying because we did not fit the profile of their normal attendee.

What they found was that OUR MISSION was to create *fundable* Borrowers. Whatever conclusions they came to, one of their liaisons contacted us and asked us who we would like to meet with at FICO®.

We were stunned.

Not only did we get to *visit* the Mount Olympus of Funding Approvals, but we were also going to be able to *meet* with members of the FICO® *Pantheon*.

Below was our response to our FICO® liaison's request:

> *"We are looking to talk to a specialist that can help us determine tactics that will create rapid improvements in a Borrower's credit profile so that they hit Lender underwriting criteria—not just get a few credit score points.*
>
> *"We have client companies who are trying to shape their business credit profiles to improve their funding capacity. We are looking to talk to a specialist that can help us determine tactics that will create improvements in these business credit profiles to increase their business credit and funding capacity. We want to also talk about SBSS℠ and how it will affect business credit optimization."*

Little did we know what amazing opportunities the FICO® Pantheon had in store for us.

April 2016 finally arrived and with high hopes, my Executive Team and I were off to FICO World. Our clear intention was to validate and improve our *current* personal Borrower Profile optimization tech AND discover how to do for *business funding* what we had mastered in the personal funding arena.

The first thing I learned when we walked into this massive convention center was that FICO®, and this entire conference, was dedicated to *optimization*—lending optimization to be precise.

It was amazing to see that our focus and commitment to optimization was similar to that of FICO®—and it was a powerful reminder that we were on the right track.

Enter Zeus

Now please remember that our clients' funding successes to this point had been significant. And as overly-confident as it may sound, it is not uncommon for me to be the smartest man in the room in any gathering or discussion about Borrower credit and funding.

However, *that* week at FICO World[2016] was a lesson in eating Humble Pie. Lots and lots of it.

After our first day of classes, Brad[5], Hannah, and I found seats at a dinner table where some of our class instructors were eating. We were poking fun at ourselves to our table companions about how little we knew, and that we were the least Lending optimization-savvy people in the room. A gentleman approached our table, sat down with us, and introduced himself as Will Lansing, the CEO of FICO®.

WTF??? Zeus of the Funding World was sitting at our table!!!

After some introductions, I was blown away by what he said next:

"Tell me about your business model."

---

[5] Brad Burnett has been my partner in this vision for the better part of 10 years and has helped me develop and prove the viability of Fundability Optimization™. Most of the ideas that we have implemented to "get the word out" about this amazing technology were introduced and implemented by him—including his insistence that I write this damn book.

I told him that where FICO® optimized *Lending*, we optimized *Borrowing*.

His countenance visibly lit up.

I explained that we helped Borrowers who were not fundable to shape their Borrower Behaviors so they could pass underwriting criteria and attract the best funding possible.

He was very intrigued, and asked some clarifying questions about our approach.

Now, I didn't know what he knew about us (it appeared he approached our table intentionally), or if he knew anything at all. What I *did* know was that we were talking to the man who could change EVERYTHING for us, for our tech, and for the future funding success of our clients.

And he did.

Beyond my wildest dream.

Facing our table companions he said, *"Let's have them meet with our score development teams."*

By this point, I was kicking my team in the shins under the table.

Two of our table companions "just happened" to be lead scientists on the personal score development team and the other was a solutions liaison with the business development team—*some of the very people we would be meeting with later.*

The 100 Questions

I told Mr. Lansing that we had prepared numerous questions before coming to the conference in case we had an opportunity to speak to FICO® team members, and asked if it would be possible to present those questions in our score developer meetings.

He approved my request, but said that the teams might not be able to answer every question in detail.

We left that table ON FIRE.

We retired to our rooms and worked late into the night reviewing and improving the questions we had prepared. We prioritized the questions we would ask and even re-worded and re-framed them to address more advanced questions about our *Fundability Optimization*™ tech.

We ended up with over 100 questions that pushed even the bounds of my team's collective knowledge.

By the next morning, we were ready.

When The Fates Are On Your Side

Dear reader, I have to humbly admit: ALL OF THIS WAS NO ACCIDENT. It couldn't have been. I'm not smart enough, aware enough, or powerful enough to have created this "confluence of circumstances" on my own.

Too many things flowed too simply, too elegantly, and too effortlessly for any of this to be random. You may be a fellow believer in this principle or you may not, but in *my* life THINGS HAPPEN FOR A REASON.

Just like you holding this book in your hands.

Just like you, I want to do the most I can to improve the world. I want all the hard work that I invested in developing and fine-tuning this amazing technology to make a difference in as many lives as possible.

Especially in the lives of you and your loved ones.

But I want you to be able to do it the easy way. That is why we have met here, in these pages, to explore how we can do it together.

Just know...you reading this book IS NO DIFFERENT than *my* crazy "random" conversation with a stranger who showed me new possibilities for what I wanted for my personal and professional life.

Your situation and my situation are very similar—we BOTH have come to realize there is *more* for us—*more* possibilities and *more* opportunities.

And, as I did at *that* moment at *that* table, *this* moment is *your* moment to take *your* business and *your* life to a whole new level.

Meeting With The FICO® Pantheon

Our FICO® Liaison (who still coordinates meetings and phone calls with FICO® team members to this day) set up several meetings over the next few days.

He also told me I'd have to sign a Non-Disclosure Agreement (NDA) to ensure that their secret-sauce remain highly-guarded.[6]

Each of these meetings allowed us to take our knowledge of *Fundability Optimization*™ to new heights and depths and allowed us to connect dots we had never connected before.

In all but one of our meetings, there was a gentleman who we affectionately called the "NDA police" whose sole purpose for being there was to verify whether or not the FICO® team members could answer my questions.

---

[6] Everything in these pages falls within the scope and bounds of my NDA.

In each meeting, I had the opportunity to ask the questions we prepared. Sometimes we got very specific answers. Sometimes we got estimations and "rounded" answers. And sometimes they said, "I can't disclose that information."

The great news for us was that these brilliant minds we were meeting with had no way of knowing what we *already* knew.

So even their "rounded" answers and estimations allowed us to read between the lines and connect new dots that let us improve our *Fundability Optimization*™ tech and increase the funding results for our clients and students.

What's fascinating is that every one of the people we met with was willing to work with us as much as they could and contribute as much as possible to our education. They were warm and welcoming in every way.

Apparently, we brought our "A" Game too. One of the FICO® team members we met with told us in one of our meetings:

> *"You're miles ahead of the competition [in the Borrower space] in terms of how you present and how you engage with your backend customers. I mean the level of engagement you've had with these guys [the FICO score development teams]—the access to these guys and the questions that you're asking—you are highly atypical. You are in rare [company]...this is Einstein level [access]."*

But why should this matter to you?

Because now YOU have "inside access" to fundability technology that is available NOWHERE ELSE. Now you have access to a valid and proven process that can make you fundable—a process whose design was influenced by the very scientists who designed the FICO® scoring system.

And now it's time you take control of *your* fundability.

Let me show you how.

Chapter 2
Why Credit Repair Sucks

Much of the positive change that has transformed our world over the ages was channeled by "disruptive" men and women who did 'time' or were in captivity.

Or worse.

Some ended up there because of their faith, others because of their out-of-the-box thinking, and others because of their folly. Socrates, the Apostles, Sir Thomas More, Galileo, Joan of Arc, Voltaire, Joseph Smith, Gandhi, Dali, Nelson Mandela, and many others. They all did time. *And the world is far better because of it...*

First of all, let's get our terms straight so we can have an intelligent conversation about a subject that, for many people, is very confusing.

The media and financial culture that surrounds "credit repair" has gotten us into some very bad habits—and trouble.

Because of these bad habits, Borrowers, Lenders, and the media tend to use terms such as "bad credit," "negative credit," "negative accounts," etc. *incorrectly.*

For example, a lien, judgment, or bankruptcy is NOT an account, but are thrown in the mix with the "late pays," the "charge-offs," and the "collections."

To make matters worse, each of the Credit Bureaus uses different references: Equifax® uses the term *derogatory account*, Experian® uses the term *negative items*, TransUnion® uses the term *negative information*, and myFICO.com uses the term *derogatory description*.

To complicate matters even more, FICO® differentiates *derogatory description* from the term *negative indicator* because the latter is used when an account is being penalized (and loses points) for some behavior, but the account itself is not derogatory.

For example, a revolving account may not be *derogatory* because it is *Paid as Agreed*, but it may have a *negative indicator* because its utilization is at 80%.

In this book, I will use the term *derogatory listing* to describe the type of information on a Borrower Profile that represents a Borrower's payment delinquency and the subsequent degradation of the account through the process of charge-off, collection, judgment, and bankruptcy.

Doing this will also help differentiate the roles of the reporting and scoring processes and the organizations that perform them.

As you have already discovered, all the Funding Game Players (plus the media) have made sure you focus your attention on the misleading notion that you can have either *good* credit or *bad* credit. As a result, you have also been led to believe (incorrectly) that the only way to "fix" bad credit is to:

1. *Wait for 7-10 years for your derogatory listings to fall off your credit report, or*

2. *Write dispute letters to the Credit Bureaus and hope some of your derogatory listings are deleted, or*

3. *Engage a credit repair company to do #2 for you.*

And if you choose #3 above, your results may be disappointing. The truth of the matter is that credit repair firms, on average, have a deletion rate of only 20-30% of the listings they dispute.

Simply put, if you have 10 derogatory items on your Profile, credit repair companies might get two or three of them deleted.

Maybe.

And if that wasn't discouraging enough, consider this...

Without knowing how valuable an account is to your Profile, credit repair companies can make your fundability even WORSE.

Think of it like this...most credit repair firms engage in what I call a "scorched earth" dispute policy. This means they attempt to delete ANY and ALL derogatory listings.

But since credit repair companies do not know what FICO® actually measures, they will delete accounts that may be adding MORE positive contribution to your Profile than negative drag against it— even if the account is labeled with a derogatory description.

Another way credit repair takes a Borrower's credit from bad to worse is by leaving customers with derogatory listings on some Bureaus but not on others.

This results in higher-than-acceptable ranges between the highest and lowest credit scores as calculated by FICO® (because the data being measured is *different* on each Bureau).

The larger the range, the less credible your Profile and the more often you will be sent to manual underwriting or denied funding.

Ignorance...Or Deception?

To make matters even worse, most credit repair companies do not offer "credit building" strategies—they just delete accounts and run.

And even if the random credit repair company does recommend credit-building techniques (like opening secured credit cards) they don't know what FICO® and the Lenders are measuring, so they ignorantly (or deceptively) recommend credit cards that prove even more destructive to a fundable Borrower Profile—while putting referral fees in their pockets.

I should know...I met lots of shady people in my credit repair days.

In 1992, I co-founded Lexington Law Firm (which today is the single largest credit repair organization in the country). I was at Lexington for five years where I helped develop and implement their credit report disputing strategies.

It was at Lexington where I began to see that causing derogatory listings to be deleted from a credit report did NOT usually make a Borrower capable of qualifying for funding approvals.

Thousands of Lexington customers were initially excited about their deletion results, but then became very discouraged when they discovered they still couldn't get approved for important purchases like auto loans, home loans, or even high-value bank credit cards.

At the time, I had no clue what it took to make a Borrower fundable.

But it was the discontent of so many customers that provided the fertile soil which allowed me to develop and grow *Fundability Optimization*™ a few years later.

Fundability Optimization™ is *the* SOLUTION to the problems and limitations created by credit repair (more on this in a later chapter).

Next-Gen Solutions

I'm asked all the time to explain the difference between *Fundability Optimization*™ and credit repair.

And my answer is always the same—the difference is vast, incomparable, radically different.

More importantly, the results created by each are radically different.

The optimization process is so advanced that to compare it to credit repair is an insult to its technological and strategic ability to create fundable Borrowers. In short:

• *Credit repair may delete a few negatives from your credit report*

- *Credit repair offers NO guarantee whether or not a derogatory listing will be deleted*

- *Implementation of Fundability Optimization™ guarantees to make you fundable and get approvals because YOU are in control*

It's like comparing a horse and buggy to a Tesla. In reality, NO legitimate comparison exists.

To Be (Or Not To Be) Fundable

The single greatest misunderstanding when it comes to the world of credit and funding is that having derogatory listings is only ONE WAY you can be un-fundable. There are numerous other ways to ruin your fundability that are never included in the *bad credit* vs. *good credit* conversation.

Each of the following "conditions" can cause funding denials, severely limit your funding approval amounts, and/or raise your interest rates:

- *Too many inquiries*

- *Too high account balances*

- *Too little credit*

- *Too short of a credit history*

- *Low-value accounts on your Profile*

- *Too much available credit*

While it may seem that there are MORE ways to be un-fundable than you first thought possible, there are significantly MORE solutions to the problem as well.

The list above sets the record straight and finally exposes many of the causes of un-fundability and puts them out in the open.

At least NOW we know what we are up against.

When you shift your focus from the misconception of *good credit* vs. *bad credit* to the idea of *fundable* vs. *not fundable,* your relationship to the Funding Game changes radically AND you open yourself to a completely new set of tools that can transform your ability to get funding.

For example, current FICO® scoring software measures approximately 40 characteristics of your Borrower Profile. These are the same 40 metrics I refer to throughout this book as *Borrower Behaviors.*[7]

Only 10 of these Borrower Behaviors measure the negative impact caused by your derogatory listings.

Sample "Borrower Behaviors"

FICO® grades **40**± characteristics of your credit profile

Only **10** measure derogatory accounts

30 ways to increase fundability and credit score regardless of derogatory accounts

CREDIT SCORE REASON FACTORS	
TransUnion (TU) - Equifax (EFX) - Experian (XPN)	
00	No adverse factor
01	Amount owed on accounts is too high
02	Level of delinquency on accounts
03	TU - Proportion of loan balances to loan amounts is too high
	EFX & XPN - Too few banks/national revolving accounts
04	TU - Lack of recent installment loan information
05	EFX & XPN - Too many bank/national revolving accounts
	Too many accounts with balances
06	Too many consumer finance company accounts
07	Account payment history is too new to rate
08	Too many inquiries last 12 months
09	Too many accounts recently opened
10	Proportion of balances to credit limits on bank/national revolving or other revolving accounts is too high
11	Amount owed on revolving accounts is too high
12	Length of time revolving accounts have been established
13	Time since delinquency is too recent or unknown
14	Length of time accounts have been established
15	Lack of recent bank/national revolving information
16	Lack of recent revolving account information
17	No recent non-mortgage balance information
18	Number of accounts with delinquency
19	TU - Date of last inquiry too recent
	EFX & XPN - Too few accounts currently paid as agreed
20	Time since derogatory public record or collection is too short
21	Amount past due on accounts
22	Serious delinquency, derogatory public record or collection filed
23	Number of bank/national revolving accounts with balances
24	No recent revolving balances
26	TU - Number of bank / national revolving or other revolving accounts
	EFX & XPN - Number of revolving accounts
27	Too few accounts currently paid as agreed

---

[7] I refer to this as the "FICO 40." We'll cover this in great detail later.

This means there are 30 Borrower Behaviors whose positive effects can be used to strategically *overwhelm* the negative "drag" against your score caused by the presence of derogatory listings on your Profile!

This is great news for Borrowers—especially those whose Borrower Behaviors have been less than perfect in the past.

Knowing this dynamic and acting on it can significantly limit the negative impact caused by your derogatory listings. The result is a more valuable and more fundable Borrower Profile.

What if you could access and learn ALL the Borrower Behaviors in the FICO® universe?[8]

Imagine the positive impact on your funding capacity if you were to implement ALL the measured behaviors.

When Score Increases Don't Matter...Even To You

Finally, there is another important difference between *Fundability Optimization*™ and credit repair. With credit repair, you give your credit report to a third party who writes disputes on your behalf. Some items may come off and your score may even go up, yet you didn't contribute ANYTHING to the improvement (or the process).

At a subtle (unconscious) level, the improvement to your score won't mean much to you.

It just happened.

It was a windfall—a freebie.

You contributed little-to-nothing in making the deletions happen, so the result may have little-to-no-value to you.

You may be happy because you think the deletions will get you approved for financing, but your happiness will be short-lived.

---

[8] In a later chapter you will learn how to access ALL of the Borrower Behaviors available for measurement by FICO®.

It will quickly disappear when you get your next credit denial. And you will be left scratching your head, wondering what happened.

Fundability Optimization™ is different.

With it, you will intentionally implement strategies and behaviors[9] that will result in positive, meaningful change.

And when you implement these behaviors and get positive feedback, you will not want to go back to your old ways again.

When you see that your new behaviors caused your fundability to improve AND resulted in significantly more funding approvals, you are going to keep doing the things that created these new and awesome results.

There is a massive payoff for establishing these new patterns and you will probably keep these habits—and the amazing fundability that comes with them—for the rest of your life.

Besides, doesn't it feel better to have control over your own results?

---

[9] These behavior changes are not radical and they don't take a lot of time—they are simple and easy. They only require a little awareness and some fine-tuning of the dials.

Chapter 3
Stop Throwing Your Damn Money Away

Why? Because one thing happened to each of them while they were confined against their will—they had the opportunity (read: forced) to think. To evaluate the world and their place in it. This new "limitation" also provided a new unforeseen "freedom"—it forced each of them into isolation from the world and an opportunity to dive deep into his or her heart, mind, and spirit.

I know. Because it happened to me...

If we compare the Funding Game to basketball, then being un-fundable is like being *benched*.

Sometimes things can happen *to you* that will make you un-fundable.

You can be benched because of a financial "injury"—like losing a job, experiencing a medical emergency, or making a mistake which results in derogatory listings on your Borrower Profile.

There are numerous situations where "shite" happens.[10]

We are not always in control of the things that happen *to us*.

For most Borrowers (maybe even you) being benched is not the result of a financial injury—but because they keep "fouling out."

Fouling out means you are not playing by the rules of the Funding Game. The problem is that until now, you didn't even know what the rules were—and Lenders certainly haven't taught them to you.

But being on the sidelines doesn't mean you have to stay there.

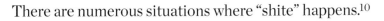

---

[10] Rumor has it that it's not swearing if you say it in another language.

Part of becoming a great Player in the Funding Game is knowing how to come back from an injury—or from fouling out. It takes determination to learn the rules of this Game, and then get back on the court when you have been benched.

One of the problems of being on the sideline is that it is costing you a small fortune—in cold hard cash and especially in loss of opportunities. Let's review three examples of what happens when you are not fundable.[11]

When Home Loan Losses Pile Up

First, let's look at the money you will throw away on a 30-year fixed loan by not being fundable.

It is significant.

With a fundable Profile, let's say you can get 4.5% interest on a $200,000 home. Your payment will be around $1,013.

30 Year Home Loan
MONEY WASTED/LOST EACH YEAR with a "non-prime" credit home loan

		100K	200K	300K	400K	500K
3.5%	Prime	$449	$898	$1,347	$1,796	$2,245
	No Loss	$449	$898	$1,347	$1,796	$2,245
4.5%	Prime + 1%	$506	$1,013	$1,520	$2,026	$2,533
	Yearly Loss	$684	$1,380	$2,076	$2,760	$3,456
5.5%	Prime + 2%	$567	$1,135	$1,703	$2,271	$2,838
	Yearly Loss	$1,416	$2,844	$4,272	$5,700	$7,116
6.5%	Prime + 3%	$632	$1,264	$1,896	$2,528	$3,160
	Yearly Loss	$2,196	$4,392	$6,588	$8,784	$10,980
7.5%	Prime + 4%	$699	$1,398	$2,097	$2,796	$3,496
	Yearly Loss	$3,000	$6,000	$9,000	$12,000	$15,012

800+ fundable profile (4.5%)

620 un-fundable profile (6.5%)

If your Profile is NOT fundable, let's say the best you can do is a loan at 6.5%. In this case, your payment is $1,264 a month. Your cost for being un-fundable is over $250 per month and $3,000 per year.

---

[11] "Fundable" means not only being capable of being approved, but also qualifying for the very highest loans and limits, and the best rates and terms available.

That represents $3,000 lost each year *on every buy and hold property you acquire.*[12]

So...over the life of each loan, you are throwing away over $90,000 that will not end up in your nest egg or benefit your loved ones.

Poof. Gone.

Auto Loans Cost You A Bundle

Next, let's look at your losses on a $30,000 auto loan.

You hear it all the time. 0% interest OAC (on approved credit).

At 0%, your principle-only payment for this loan would be $500 per month. If your un-fundable Profile forces you to accept a 7% loan, your payment will be $594 a month, instead of $500! That's nearly $100 you are crumpling up and setting on fire EACH MONTH.

To twist the knife further, you are throwing away $5,640 over the life of that 5-year loan.

So...what could you do with a few thousand more dollars?

Flush Your Hard-Earned Money Away

And for our final scenario, let's say you are paying $1,000 per month for rent because your Profile is un-fundable.

That's $12,000 flushed down the toilet each year.

More importantly, let's assume the homes in your area are appreciating at least 5% per year.

That's another $5,000 per year you're losing on a $100,000 home.

---

[12] And if you can't get a Fannie/Freddie loan and have to resort to hard money or private money, your losses will be even more substantial.

In this scenario, you're throwing away $17,000 every single year because you are NOT fundable!

Monthly Rent	$ Lost Each Year in Rent	Lost Appreciation on $100K Home @ 5%	Total Annual $ Lost While Renting
$600	$7,200	$5,000	$12,200
$800	$9,600	$5,000	$14,600
$1,000	$12,000	$5,000	$17,000
$1,500	$18,000	$5,000	$23,000
$2,000	$24,000	$5,000	$29,000

Sadly, these losses are small in comparison to what you will lose each year if you are renting a home that is worth $200K, or $300K or more.

This is what being un-fundable is costing you. And this cost is far more than you can afford to pay.

But what is the root cause of being un-fundable?

Ignorance.

Ignorance is the most expensive condition of all—especially when it's not your fault.

It really sucks to be sitting on the bench *watching* the Game, instead of on the court *playing* it.

But there is hope...

And opportunity.

Here you will learn the rules of the Funding Game so you can get on the court, stop fouling out, and play like a Pro.

Chapter 4
Your Inner Animal: Behaviors Don't Lie

My time "inside" provided me an opportunity to do just that. Focus on me. The isolation, the loneliness, the scarce rations, and the primitive conditions allowed for only one thing— time with myself in deep contemplation. And while I do not rank myself with the great minds and hearts that have changed the world, I do hold myself as a peer in one way—I too was forced to contemplate the nature of my world and in so doing, I discovered a few small (and maybe significant) ways I could help inspire evolution and change within my realm of influence...

Just like Lenders developed survival strategies to cope with their beliefs about Borrowers, Borrowers have developed survival strategies to cope with their beliefs about Lenders.

These survival strategies are the *beliefs* and *behaviors* handed down to us from our parents, families, communities, and society—for generations. And because they were passed down to us from others, we implement them UNCONSCIOUSLY. We automatically believe they are true, and yet we have never examined them for ourselves.

The challenge is that FICO® and Lender approval software are DESIGNED to track, measure, and evaluate your Borrower Behaviors. Lenders want to know, MORE THAN ANYTHING ELSE, how you treat loans, credit cards, and credit lines that have been (or are currently) extended to you.

The System is *counting on you* to behave UNCONSCIOUSLY.

They believe they can only trust the data they collect about you *if you are not aware* of what is being measured. This chapter will let you examine your unconscious behaviors, so you can begin to behave *intentionally* and *consciously*. To help you become aware of our unconscious beliefs and the Borrower Behaviors that are the result, let's use the characteristics of animals as an analogy.

Let's take a look at what I like to call "Borrower Totems."

These totems reflect your unconscious beliefs and behaviors about money and borrowing—especially how you treat OPM from financial institutions.

In the next few pages, I will describe several of these financial totems and I want you to determine which animal(s) represent your attitudes, beliefs and behaviors towards Other People's Money.

These totems represent negative behaviors. I do not present them here to criticize you—just to create awareness to make you fundable.

Remember, there is a MEASURABLE reason why you are not fundable. Open your heart and your mind and be willing to explore this with me. You can only get "there" by knowing where "here" is.

When you bring these behaviors to your active, deliberate, and conscious awareness, only then can you change them. And when you change your Borrower Behaviors, you will change your fundability.

The Ostrich

Ostriches are avoiders.

"Don't tell me about my situation."

"I don't want to know anything."

""I can't look at my bills right now."

"I don't want to look at my credit report because it's bad."

"I don't want to apply for funding because I know I will be denied."

Ostriches want to avoid looking at their current financial or credit circumstances. Some go even as far as avoiding learning how to improve their situation.

The fact that you are reading this book indicates that you are willing to explore the truth of your situation and do something about it.

The Rat

Rats are shrewd and financially crafty. Rats perceive they *need* OPM to "make it" and will take any credit at any cost.

Many times, Rats act like *any* credit offer is a *good* offer.

They are likely to be someone who opens their mail and says, "Oh look! Someone pre-approved me for a credit card. I could use that money...I should apply!"

Rats don't know why they've received those credit offers, much less how those offers will negatively impact their funding opportunities.

They aren't aware that responding to those offers will downgrade their fundability and ruin future high-value funding opportunities.

The Ram

Isolated, alone, on the craggy cliffs of life, Rams have no connection with the financial system—they want nothing to do with the Funding Game. Some isolationists became such because they got hurt or burned financially.

Others avoid the system because they are not confident in their ability to play this Game, so they react with:

"I'm debt-free, cash only."

At conferences where I am speaking, I get people who come up to me and say, *"I don't need credit to do deals."*

"That may be true," I reply, *"But if you took all of your vast intelligence and capability as an investor and leveraged really inexpensive bank money, you would have even more success than you have now."*

Playing the Funding Game like a Pro means LEVERAGING OPM.

The Chicken

Chickens spend their lives looking down at the ground, scratching out a living— usually within a very narrow view of the world. *"I just want to make ends meet."*

This is how many Borrowers act who live paycheck-to-paycheck. These are the Borrowers who are discouraged because their income barely covers their expenses. They don't have a lot of opportunity yet to build a life of prosperity.

Chickens are a little afraid and have a very short-term focus. *"I'll be fine if I can just get through this week."*

The Fox

Foxes are schemers. *"I do what I can to take advantage of the system."*

"If it's a Game—I'm gonna cheat."

These are the Borrowers who think, *"I'm going to get any credit I can, I'm going to try and make money with it...but if something goes wrong, I'll walk away from it and fix my credit later."*

FICO® and Lenders do not want Foxes in their henhouse. To prevent it, they have designed their algorithms to detect abusive Borrower Behaviors.

Personally, if I encounter a Fox who wants to be a student or client, I won't allow it. I don't work with these types of Borrowers.[13]

We're not here to cheat anybody. We're here to learn how to play the Funding Game and be Pros at it. We are here to create a mutually-profitable partnership with Lenders.

The Sheep

Sheep are "followers" with a mindset that relies on external authority and the opinions of others.

"Don't mind me. I'm just going to hang out in the crowd unnoticed."

"I just do what I'm told."

"A real estate agent told me to shop around for a home loan, so I did."

"My auto dealer told me he needed to pull my credit a lot, so I let him."

"My banker told me I should open a check guarantee card with my account, so I let him."[14]

The good news is that by you investing time into exploring the principles in these pages, you are not just following the crowd.

I applaud your commitment to *find* out the truth for yourself and then *implement* what you have learned.

---

[13] If you're reading this to see what you can do to game the system, STOP. You are wasting your time.

[14] More on this subject later.

The Seagull

Seagulls are different from Rats. Rather than sneaking around to get what they want, they are more bold and brash about their borrowing strategies. Seagulls tend to believe that money is scarce—that there is not enough to go around.

As a result, they may be envious of the success of others and tend to compete, rather than collaborate, to be successful. They may fight for what they can get—even if what they are fighting for are scraps.

Whether we like it or not, FICO® and Lender underwriting software are designed to detect *EVERY ONE OF THESE BEHAVIORS*.

In future chapters, I will refer back to these Borrower Totems and point out important Borrower Behaviors to watch for.

Reality Check

So? How did you do? Did you relate to one or more of the Borrower Totems?

Did you find yourself defending against or avoiding how true one or more of these Borrower Totems might be for you?

When you recognized (maybe reluctantly) which behaviors you may relate to, you probably felt some discomfort.

This is good news!

Becoming aware of your Borrower Totems allows you to recognize the origins of the financial survival strategies you have used to cope with financial stress your whole life.

And without knowing it, these beliefs leave us hiding from the truth, scurrying to grab what we can, following the herd, picking at the leftovers, or even walking away from the Game completely.

It's like you inherited a car from your parents that is only using 10% of its horsepower and, because you don't know any different, you drive it around clueless of its full potential.

Your willingness to honestly look at yourself is the first step in changing EVERYTHING. Reading this book is proof that you are not content living your life from your survival strategies.

You are ready to *know* and *act* CONSCIOUSLY. You want to lead yourself and loved ones to a better life. You want to create happiness, wealth, and success.

If we're not expanding, we're contracting, right?

Each of these Borrower Totems represents some form of fear.

But maybe you are afraid because you are not confident at how well you are playing the Funding Game—and no one taught you how.

Here, you are learning rules of the Funding Game.

If you know how to play this Game, if you know what you're doing, you will never have to be afraid again:

- *You will know what it takes to get approved.*

- *You will know how to create a post-bankruptcy soft landing.*

- *You will know how to navigate a divorce or partnership dissolution without letting finances contribute to this already difficult and painful process.*

Every time you implement one of the insider strategies in this book, you will create greater mastery of the Funding Game.

And greater success in your funding approvals.

So what is the alternative to these "negative" Borrower Totems? Which animal would reflect a positive set of Borrower Behaviors and represent you as a Professional Borrower?

The Eagle

Eagles act from clarity, intention, and purpose. They are powerful, strategic, and proactive. If you have vision and focus...you are an Eagle.

Your goal here is to become a Professional Borrower—a Pro at playing the Funding Game.

Acting from a place of *conscious awareness* of the behaviors that will put OPM in your pocket *is the very essence* of a Funding Eagle.

While the beliefs represented by your *unconscious* Borrower Totems may have helped you survive financially in the past, only the conscious beliefs and behaviors of The Eagle will help you thrive, prosper, and create a life you LOVE living.

The next chapters will show you how to transform your understanding of how the Funding Game works and use your new understanding to create more and better opportunities for your life and loved ones.

But that isn't all.

Even if you are now aware of your unconscious financial behaviors...

And even if you are committed to going all in and becoming a Funding Eagle and playing the Game like a Pro...

To be successful, you must also know who the other Players are and how THEY play the Game.

Chapter 5
Why You're Getting Your Funding Ass Handed To You

> *I was prepared to do my time—three years and six months to be exact (with good behavior). But as I looked to the future at what seemed like an eternity until my release in December 2004, I was forced to get real with myself. Never before had I taken the time to meditate or get quiet and look at my life.*
>
> *For 40 years, I had been a human "doing," not a human being. And since my situation made it so there was nothing I could do to distract myself with things OUTSIDE of me, this "time-out" forced me to go INSIDE. For the first time in my life, I got to explore the depths of my soul, my values, my priorities, my motivations, and the beliefs and behaviors that created for me a prosperous life AND those that ultimately landed me in jail...*

It's time now to explore the other participants in the Funding Game. These other Players are multi-billion dollar organizations and industries—each with a mission to make as much money from you as possible.

The Players

Four major processes comprise the the Funding Game—and each is performed by a DIFFERENT PLAYER:

- ***Borrowers*** *BORROW funds and exhibit their Borrower Behaviors*

- ***Credit Bureaus*** *COLLECT then REPORT Borrower Behaviors*

- ***FICO®*** *INTERPRETS and SCORES 40± Borrower Behaviors*

- ***Lenders*** *EVALUATE Borrower Behavior and scores to determine whether or not to approve a Borrower's funding requests*

Understanding the relationship between each of these Players and how they relate to YOU is vital. Let's take a look at each of them to see how they contribute to the Funding Game.

Borrowers

Of the four Players, the most important is The Borrower. Our entire financial system fails when Borrowers do not borrow. And yet, Borrowers do not realize this and therefore believe they are at the mercy of all the other Players.

And until you become a Professional Borrower and learn how to play the Funding Game well, you will be treated with little-to-no respect from the other Players.

It is not uncommon to hear Borrowers complain about how Lenders treat them. Most feel they are "just a number" and have no influence with these ALL POWERFUL institutions.

And it's TRUE—unless you change it.

Because until YOU change the paradigm and play the Funding Game like their PEER—like a Pro—Lenders are unlikely to take you seriously.

Until YOU start acting differently, YOU will only be their prey, their meal ticket, their source of income.

YOU have to *level-up* and *improve* how YOU play the Game.

And it's easy when you know how.

Lenders

Lenders include any institution that lends you money. Lenders, old or new, play by the rules of a Game that is over 500 years old—borrowing Other People's Money at low rates and lending THE SAME MONEY at higher rates.[15]

---

[15] Example: Bank pays depositors 2% and lends money to the SAME depositor for a credit card, auto or home loan at 5-25%. Knowing how to profit within the spread IS the Funding Game.

Credit Bureaus

Next we have the Credit Bureaus. Legally they are known as consumer reporting agencies (CRAs) and have been collecting and reporting Borrower Behaviors for over 90 years.

There are lots of different consumer reporting agencies.[16]

So for clarity, we are going to use the term "Credit Bureaus" to distinguish them from all the agencies which also report on consumers.

FICO®

The last of the Players is Fair Issac Corporation (FICO®). FICO® has been grading the fundability of Borrower Behaviors for over 70 years—and getting better and more precise at it every year.[17]

The Game

Given this new level of awareness, let's review how these Players interact.

When a Borrower submits a funding application, the Lender sends an inquiry to one, two, or all three Credit Bureaus to get current and historical Borrower Behavior data.[18]

This Borrower Behavior data is formatted and delivered as a *credit report*.

---

[16] Other CRAs include medical record reporters, resident and tenant history reporters, check-writing reporters, and criminal and public record reporters.

[17] As of this printing, FICO® announced the 2020 release of FICO® Score 10 which will include the same unweighted and industry-specific scores available in previous versions of their scoring software.

[18] Also known as a credit "pull," inquiries come in two forms: a "hard" inquiry and a "soft" inquiry. A hard pull gives a Lender complete access to the contents of your Profile and counts against your credit score for 12 months and against your fundability for 24 months. Alternately, a soft pull allows a Lender to see only key data points—including your FICO® Score—to review your account. Soft inquiries do not negatively affect your score or fundability.

A credit report is a *document* that reports both a Borrower's *current* Profile[19] AND any previous accounts that are now closed.[20]

The Bureau databases have FICO® software embedded in their mainframes that grade a Borrower's Profile IN REAL TIME.

This is different than what we have been led to believe.

Until now, most of us have believed that we have "A CREDIT SCORE" as though there is only *one.*

It is common for us to ask, *"What's my credit score?"*

This question promotes another common misconception.

There is no single STATIC credit score that resides on Credit Bureau databases. Scores are real-time, dynamic ratings that are calculated on the fly.

Not only do your credit scores CHANGE ALL THE TIME, but you can also have numerous DIFFERENT scores based on which

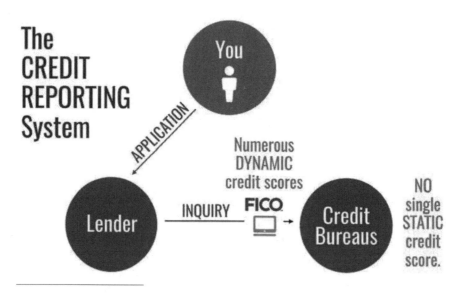

The CREDIT REPORTING System

You

APPLICATION

Numerous DYNAMIC credit scores

INQUIRY FICO

Lender

Credit Bureaus

NO single STATIC credit score.

---

[19] A Borrower Profile is the portfolio of all open accounts currently reported by Lenders.

[20] Open accounts stay on your credit report indefinitely. Closed positive accounts stay on your credit report for 10 years from the date of closure.

Bureau/Version of FICO® software is being used to evaluate (filter) your Borrower Behaviors (more on this in a later chapter).

Regardless of which software is doing the evaluating, these dynamic credit scores are calculated the moment the inquiry is submitted.

After your data is filtered by the FICO® algorithms and scoring software, it is delivered to the Lender electronically in the form of a credit report.

When the Lender receives your Borrower Profile data, it is filtered through the Lender's custom underwriting software where it is graded against internal proprietary funding guidelines.

This is known as *automatic underwriting* (this is very important).

If your application data, FICO® evaluation and score, and Bureau data fit the Lender guidelines, you are approved.

Automatic underwriting can take less than 30 seconds to notify you of an approval or denial.

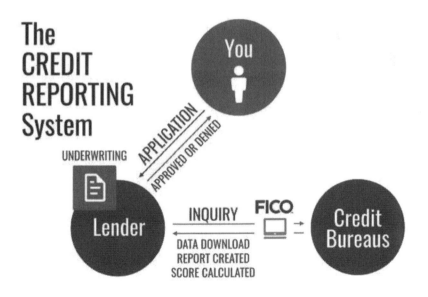

If it takes longer, you can be confident that your application triggered yellow and/or red flags and was sent to manual underwriting to be reviewed in greater detail—usually by a human.

If you are reading between the lines here, you may notice that I have barely mentioned your credit score in this process.

In truth, your credit score may rank 3rd or 4th in importance when evaluating your data for approval—depending on what you are applying for. Automatic underwriting systems (AUS) place more importance on *other* criteria.

We will explore this in greater detail in a later chapter, but you must understand that the very SCORE you have been programmed to pay attention to is NOT usually the most important thing *Lenders* pay attention to.

Your score is only one of many criteria that Lenders use when seeking to approve your application.

As you will learn shortly, the MOST important thing they evaluate is your Borrower Behavior—what FICO® and Lenders call your performance data.

To bring it full circle...once you are approved and you make a payment, that new account gets reported to the Credit Bureaus by the Lender, and your Borrower Behavior with this account starts being tracked as well.

 The circle of "Funding Life" begins anew.

In the next chapter, I'm going to reveal one of the biggest lies perpetrated on 80+ million Borrowers across this country.

And they don't even know it.

Could you be one of them?

Chapter 6

The Truth? The Whole Truth? Nothing But The Truth?

Before my "time-out," I had every appearance of success. I had three amazing children, a thriving business, and a fun and adventurous life. But what started as an adventure began to career out of control. This is not the place to go into the epicurean hedonism that was my life at the time but, suffice to say, I went to prison because of my folly. I was arrested for possession of a controlled substance (ecstasy) in the proximity of firearms (legal and registered). I learned too late the proximity of the two is a no-no...

As you learned in the *Introduction*, one of the three major strategies used by Lenders to protect their interests is to distract Borrowers from what is being measured by getting them fixated on their credit score.

And as the next three chapters will reveal, they have done a spectacular job of it. To set the stage, you must answer this question:

Are all credit scores created equal?

No. They are not.

One of the major components of the misinformation campaign promoted by the Players in the Funding Game is the use of credit scores that have NOTHING to do with Lender funding approvals.

To understand what has been happening behind your back, you need to know what each type of fake credit score is and how it is used so that you don't get distracted by or lost down the credit score "rabbit hole."

In short, there are FICO® scores, and there are Fake-O™ scores.[21]

---

[21] The industry refers to these as "educational" scores. I use the term Fake-O™ to emphasize their fake and deceptive nature.

FICO® Scores

FICO® is the gold standard in Borrower Behavior scoring. Over 90% of ALL funding decisions are evaluated using FICO® scoring[22] software.

This fact makes the meetings we had at FICO® even more meaningful. We had the rare opportunity to sit with, and ask high-level questions of, the teams responsible for creating the engine that facilitates most funding decisions!

And the intel we got from those meetings was game-changing.

In the next chapter, we will unlock the FICO® credit scoring universe into easy-to-understand pieces. But first, let's explore the "shiny object" of Fake-O™ scores.

Fake-O™ Scores

I define a score that is offered or sold to Borrowers but is NOT typically used by Lenders to make a funding decision a Fake-O™ score.

And there are a bunch of them.

Fake-O™ scores were designed to profit from the ignorance of Borrowers by leading Borrowers to believe that the credit scores being offered were legitimate.[23]

Let's explore how Fake-O™ scores were first invented.

In 1996, Congress amended the Fair Credit Reporting Act (FCRA) because the Credit Bureaus were doing a horrible job of managing and accurately reporting the Borrower Profiles on their databases.

---

[22] What is commonly (and inaccurately) referred to as "credit scoring" is technically referred to by FICO® and Lenders as "performance data" scoring and which I refer to as "Borrower Behavior" scoring.

[23] Due to recent lawsuits, many Fake-O™ score issuers must include disclaimers (in fine print) warning Borrowers that their advertised scores are NOT used in funding decisions. Because Borrowers are kept in the dark regarding the rules of the Funding Game, many can read the disclaimers and still not know what it means—or how it will affect them.

Numerous public interest groups and consumer advocates had proven to Congress that over 60% of credit reports contained mistakes that would cause a credit denial.

The FCRA was amended to order the Credit Bureaus to provide one free copy of "all data maintained and reported" to Borrowers every year—upon request.

They called the file containing all reported Bureau data a "consumer disclosure file."

This was not to be a typical "credit report" because it would contain ALL the "raw data" kept and reported by the Bureaus.

The language in the amendment was specific in that it dictated if a Bureau reported the data to ANYONE, it would have to be included in this disclosure file.

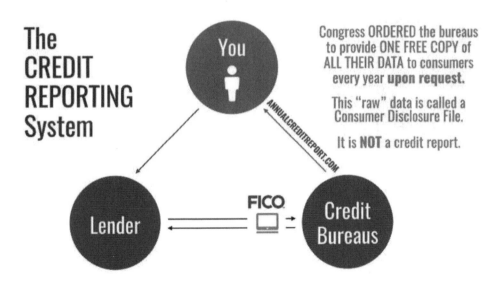

The Credit Bureaus were also instructed to establish a single access point where a Borrower could get this consumer disclosure file.

In response, the Credit Bureaus created *AnnualCreditReport.com*

To this day, this website serves as the place where Borrowers can get a complete disclosure of all information reported by the Credit Bureaus.

How Do We Make Money?

This mandate from Congress did not sit well with the Credit Bureaus. Providing this new consumer disclosure file had become a huge cost for them.

Imagine the conversation in the respective boardrooms of Equifax®, Experian®, and TransUnion®...

> *"How can we make money from this Congressional mandate AND NOT have to disclose all of this valuable data?"*

The Credit Bureaus NEVER lack for finding ways to make money. Their lobbyists had inserted a loophole in the amended FCRA that allowed Credit Bureaus to reduce the data delivered to a Borrower if the Borrower opted for a different product during the order process.

To *increase* their profits and legally *withhold* their data, the Credit Bureaus decided that when Borrowers ordered their disclosure files, they would ask a simple question:

> *"Would you like a credit score with your order?"*

The rationale was that a credit score is a function of a *credit report* and NOT part of a *consumer disclosure file*. At the click of a button, a comprehensive disclosure file would become an abbreviated credit report containing far fewer data points AND a fake score.[24]

Without realizing the manipulation, Borrowers would be maneuvered into ordering a credit report because the Borrower would be distracted by the "shiny object" of a credit score— something Borrowers never had access to before.

---

[24] Consumer disclosures files are not "score-able" in their raw-data format. To convert the data into a credit report, it had to be filtered into a score-able format which allowed the Credit Bureaus to NOT include all the data.

This ruse allowed Credit Bureaus to legally withhold much of the raw data that would otherwise be available to Borrowers.

To implement this strategy the Credit Bureaus (among others) simply invented fake scores and offered them to Borrowers.

This was an easy scheme to execute because Borrowers had never had access to credit scores before and they wouldn't know that these fake scores were completely different from the REAL ones being used to make lending decisions.

And Fake-O™ scores were born.

When Ignorance Is NOT Bliss

The implementation of these Fake-O™ scores was followed by a media blitz that would leverage Borrower ignorance and deceive millions into believing that these "free credit scores" were not only real, but were also the most important factor in credit approvals.[25]

This was the first time that the Credit Bureaus (and others) sought to imitate the legitimate Borrower scores FICO® had been using for decades to evaluate Borrowers.

In summary, Fake-O™ score providers were able to exploit this opportunity because of two conditions:

• *Borrowers did not really know what a credit score was, how it was calculated, or how it was really used in lending decisions.*

• *Real FICO® scores were not being offered to Borrowers.*[26]

---

[25] This blitz is illustrated by the prime-time television ads of the man playing the guitar and singing about his credit woes: a girlfriend with bad credit, being forced to get a low-budget car or ride a bike, and being a victim of identity theft. Each ad implied that if you ordered their credit report and score (Fake-O™), your quality of life would improve dramatically. Web search: "Free Credit Report Commercials" to see for yourself.

[26] This silence left a vacuum for less scrupulous organizations to take advantage of Borrower ignorance. For decades, FICO®'s domain was in the background helping Lenders with intelligent approval decisioning. It wouldn't be for several more years that FICO® would start offering Borrowers access to real scores used by Lenders in their approval process.

Access to a credit score (fake as it was) was nevertheless mind-blowing to Borrowers. Up to that point, Borrowers had never had access to credit scores.

In fact for decades, Borrowers had been told by merchants and retailers that it was "illegal" to even show Borrowers their scores.[27]

With these new score offerings, Borrowers were deceptively led to believe they finally had access to the inner workings of the credit system.

Unfortunately, because of FICO®'s silence, Borrowers were left with only fake and irrelevant versions of a credit score.

Because Borrowers didn't know that the scores they were buying were meaningless, credit score sales skyrocketed and dozens of "credit report wholesalers" began offering these worthless credit scores.

Credit Bureaus make their money from selling data. And selling Borrower data in the form of a credit report to a company that wants to re-sell credit reports and fake scores is right in their wheelhouse.

The Bureaus didn't care that the reports were substandard and the accompanying scores were lies.

---

[27] While not illegal, revealing a credit score to a Borrower was a violation of Credit Bureau policy and a merchant caught doing so could jeopardize its relationship with the Credit Bureau. Today, this policy is not regularly enforced due to the easy access a Borrower has via myFICO.com to the very scores that were once hidden from Borrowers.

The Biggest "Bait And Switch" Of All Time

Guess who promotes a Fake-O™ score to over 80,000,000 unsuspecting and trusting Borrowers?

Credit Karma®.

Credit Karma® uses VantageScore® 3.0 scores on its website. This model is used mostly for account *reviews* and for "goodwill" purposes. Generally, it is NOT used for most new funding *approvals* performed in the United States.[28]

But the irony of this deception doesn't stop there.

Most of the loans and credit cards that Credit Karma® refers its members to utilize FICO® software for their approvals.

Now THAT is a bait and switch.

It is unconscionable that there are 80+ million people being misled to inaccurately judge the health of their funding approval capacity based on a credit score Lenders are unlikely to use to approve their funding applications!

This travesty is even more harmful in light of the fact that Borrowers tie their personal and financial "worthiness" to a number THAT ISN'T EVEN ACCURATE!

And while Credit Karma may be the largest promoter of fake scores, there are another 10+ million subscribers to other credit monitoring services that also offer fake scores.

Credit Karma at least offers its fake credit scores for free. Borrowers who subscribe to these other services are paying good money every

[28] VantageScore® is a scoring model designed by an organization sponsored by Equifax®, TransUnion®, and Experian® to compete against FICO® dominance in the scoring space. While VantageScore® has some models that are offered for Lender decisioning support, mostly it is used to pre-screen applicants and to manage existing accounts (if used at all). See page 1 of the 2019 VANTAGESCORE MARKET STUDY REPORT published by Oliver Wyman or my podcast on this topic for more info: GetFundablePodcast.com

month for fake scores and mediocre credit reports. And the negative impact of this deception on Borrowers has been devastating.

Now that you know the difference between FICO® and Fake-O™ scores, I'm going to pull the curtains back on how scoring really works with real FICO® scores.

Chapter 7
The FICO® Gods: Gatekeepers Of Fundability

While the activities leading up to my incarceration may spark curiosity in some, what is important to me now is not why I went to prison, but the amazing gift and opportunity it became to get on a path of self-discovery—a journey to discover who I was AND a journey to discover my purpose in the world...

As your fundability coach, I'm calling a time out.

How are you doing?

Feeling a little excited?

Overwhelmed?

Creating and maintaining your fundability definitely requires more than just magic. But I promise it's worth it.

And you are not alone. I'm on this path with you too.

Many of my students and clients have been exactly where you are right now—a little overwhelmed and maybe even a little confused.

But I promise that if you hang in there and learn how this works, you will be able to experience more funding success than you ever dreamed possible.

In the last chapter, we discussed the invention of fake scoring models which allowed unscrupulous organizations to prey on the ignorance of Borrowers and cash in on the growing awareness of the availability of credit scores—fake as they were.

These fake credit "scoreboards" made it impossible for most Borrowers to know how well they were playing the Funding Game.

That is like playing a game where the real scoreboard is hidden, and the scoreboard that you are relying on is a sign held up by some random person in the stands.

How would you REALLY know how well you were doing?

How would you REALLY know if you were winning?

In this chapter, you will discover exactly how the REAL scoreboard works—and how to know when you are playing well.

FICO® has the ONLY real scoreboard. It is the only scoreboard that Lenders use to facilitate over 90% of all funding approvals.

And the stats it keeps directly impacts your fundability.

So, if you understand how FICO® uses their scoring models to evaluate you, YOU will have the intel to shape your Borrower Behaviors to fit what they are measuring.[29]

Let's take a look now at the complete suite of FICO® credit scoring models available to Borrowers on myFICO.com. With this knowledge, you will be able to use this information to your benefit AND radically improve your fundability.

FICO® Comes To The "Credit Score" Rescue

Seeing the proliferation of fake scores, FICO® established myFICO.com in 2001 and began offering real FICO® scores to Borrowers nationwide. At first, myFICO.com offered one score.

But as the years passed, FICO® began to see the value of an informed and educated Borrower base and began offering several industry-specific Lender scores as well.[30]

---

[29] To better apply what you will learn in this chapter, I highly recommend you order your myFICO.com credit reports. The "Advanced" plan will provide the intel you need to begin your fundability optimization.

[30] These industry-specific scores were introduced to Borrowers on myFICO.com around 2015. The decision to offer these scores to Borrowers was a significant step towards providing Borrowers with information to become more fundable.

As you learned earlier, FICO® focuses its vast intelligence and financial resources to predict Borrower Behavior. In the funding space, FICO® uses its predictive analytics to *optimize* the lending process.

Let's put some context to this.

To Borrowers, FICO® is most known for their "credit" scores. But there is more to it than that.

To put it simply, FICO® has developed software to help Lenders at each stage of the funding approval process—each with its own score.

FICO® provides Lenders an Application Score,[31] a Revenue Score,[32] Fraud Scores,[33] PreScores,[34] and most recently the Small Business Scoring Service (SBSS℠) also known as LiquidCredit® Decision Engine.[35]

While not important to our discussion here, FICO® also offers scoring models for other markets—each with the full weight and force of their predictive analytics engines. There are Insurance Scores, Healthcare Scores, Property Insurance Scores, Debt Management Solutions, Collection Scores, and even a Mortgage Pricing Score.

The take-home message from all of this is that FICO® dominates the "big data" and "predictive analytics" spaces.

---

[31] The Application Score measures the difference between the information a Borrower puts on a funding request application and the Borrower data on file at the Credit Bureaus and other verification databases.

[32] The Revenue Score predicts the amount of revenue a Lender can anticipate given a Borrower's credit score and zip code.

[33] The Fraud Score works in conjunction with FICO® Falcon® Fraud Prevention Platform which monitors funding requests and transactions for fraud.

[34] As the name implies, the PreScore™ service helps Lenders evaluate whether a Lender should extend a Borrower a "pre-qualified" offer of credit. Lots more on this later.

[35] The SBSS℠ scoring model delivered by LiquidCredit® is the FICO® strategy for dominating the business credit scoring space and is fast replacing antiquated and ineffective business scoring models like Paydex® and Intelliscore®.

This fact makes the time we spent with the FICO® teams even more important. Everything you are learning in these pages is NOT AVAILABLE anywhere else and *Fundability Optimization™* tech is a game-changer for you and your financial ambitions.

The FICO® Credit Score Universe

While there are dozens of scoring products currently offered by FICO®, we will focus on the credit scores available to Borrowers on the myFICO.com website.

One or more of these scores are used to facilitate the evaluation of EVERY personal funding application you will ever submit to a Lender that uses FICO® scores.[36] Therefore, understanding the importance of what makes up these scores will drastically improve your funding success.

Each of these FICO® scores measure the same 40± Borrower Behaviors that end up recorded on a Borrower's Profile.[37]

Currently, there are a total of 28 scores offered on myFICO.com.[38] There are several factors used to create the array of myFICO.com credit scores. These include:

• *Credit Bureau data used*

• *Software version used*

• *Weighted vs. Unweighted*

The insider secret is that the *relationship* between these factors has a huge impact on your fundability. Each of the variables listed above can cause big differences between your scores.

---

[36] FICO® LiquidCredit® even uses one or more of your personal scores when evaluating your business funding requests.

[37] While FICO® calls these Borrower Behaviors "Reason Codes," for simplicity's sake, I will refer to them as the FICO® 40.

[38] It is anticipated that myFICO.com will offer the entire FICO® 10 Suite to Borrowers after its general release to Lenders. This would raise the number of available scores to at least 31.

Let's take a deeper look into these relationships.

Credit Bureau Data Used

FICO® uses the data from each Credit Bureau to formulate a corresponding score for *that* Bureau. If there are differences between the account data on file at each of the Credit Bureaus, there will also be differences between the scores that FICO® calculates.

These differences can be slight, but without implementing optimization strategies, they are usually significant.

Knowing what differences to look for and how to find them will help you to audit and optimize what the Credit Bureaus are reporting and, in turn, optimize the range between your Credit Bureau scores.

I call this *Bureau Score Optimization.*[39]

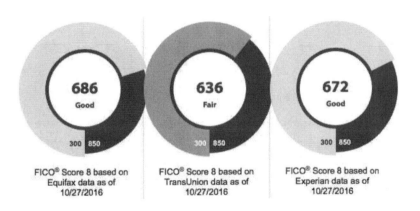

FICO® Score 8 based on Equifax data as of 10/27/2016	FICO® Score 8 based on TransUnion data as of 10/27/2016	FICO® Score 8 based on Experian data as of 10/27/2016

In the preceding illustration, there is a range of 50 points between the highest and lowest Credit Bureau Score (EQ vs. TU). The lower the range the better your fundability.

A range of 0 to 10 points is optimal.

---

[39] In my Bootcamps, I may refer to this as "horizontal" optimization because myFICO.com credit reports list each score horizontally by Credit Bureau. To optimize your scores by Credit Bureau is to reduce the range horizontally between scores.

FICO® Software Versions Used

Over the decades, FICO® has continued to update and improve their scoring software. With each new update, the predictive power of their scoring models has increased significantly.

There are four score versions published by FICO® but only three are currently available on myFICO.com. In their current form, these versions are referred to as:

- *FICO® 5-4-2. This version was introduced in 1991 providing scoring solutions that were custom-designed for each Credit Bureau: (5) for Equifax®, (4) for TransUnion®, and (2) for Experian®. In fact, all home loan approvals in this country are still using this 30-year-old version of FICO®'s software.*

- *FICO® 8. This version was released in 2009 and was the first version to consolidate the scoring model into one comprehensive version rather than have specific software for each Bureau.*

- *FICO® 9. Released in 2014, this version radically changed how collection accounts (among other things) were evaluated (especially medical collections).*

- *FICO® 10. Released in 2020, this version is being hailed as the most predictive version yet and its use will significantly reduce Lender losses from default.* [40]

Each new software release, however, presents Lenders with a dilemma. While each new version of FICO® software has greater predictive capability, it is also very costly for Lenders to install the new software across their vast networks and branches.

This dilemma has resulted in a serious mess for Borrowers. Across the vast Lender landscape, thousands of Lenders are pulling FICO® scores from *different* Credit Bureaus, using *different* versions of the

---

[40] From its January 2020 announcement, FICO® states that Lenders could reduce the number of defaults in their portfolio by as much as 10% among bankcards, 9% among auto loans, and 17% among home loans compared to earlier versions.

scoring software, and using *different* industry-specific scores. The situation is so out of control that in some cases, the scoring software used by a single Lender may even vary by state and branch.

Of course, FICO® would love to have every Lender using the most recent (and most predictive) version of its scoring software—but that is not going to happen any time soon.

This scoring "diversity" wreaks havoc with Borrowers. When completing an application, a Borrower will not know which Credit Bureau a Lender will pull nor which version of the FICO® scoring software will be used to filter and evaluate their fundability.

FICO® has included its software versions and corresponding scores on their myFICO.com credit reports as part of the scores they offer.

But unfortunately, they don't offer any significant education as to what each of the scores are, how they are calculated, how they are used, or a list of Lenders who use them.

As with the score differences between Credit Bureaus, optimizing your Borrower Profile to meet Lender funding guidelines will decrease the range between your score *versions*.

I call this *Version Score Optimization.*[41]

Equifax Difference: 31 points	675	672	635	FICO® v. 5, 4, 2
TransUnion Difference: 56 points	671	639	653	FICO® v. 8
Experian Difference: 66 points	702	616	701	FICO® v. 9

---

[41] I sometimes refer to this as "vertical" optimization because myFICO.com credit reports list each credit score vertically by version. To optimize your scores by version is to reduce the range vertically between scores.

Take a look at the preceding illustration. You will see that there are significant point differences between the highest and lowest scores as calculated by the various versions of the software.

What you must understand is that there is NO DIFFERENCE in the *data* being scored. All three software versions are using the same data as reported by each respective Bureau.

The score differences are due SOLELY to the software version being used to score the data.

That is why *Version Score Optimization* is important. You want your Profile to be fundable REGARDLESS of which software version is being used to evaluate it. The lower the range the better.

A range of 0 to 10 points is optimal.

FICO® Weighted Industry-Specific Scoring Models

The final factor that contributes to the myFICO.com score offerings is the difference between what is known as *weighted* and *unweighted* scores.

Let's look at *weighted* scores first.

Earlier you learned that FICO® added *industry-specific* scores on myFICO.com a few years ago. Each is designed to evaluate a specific credit account type as offered by different industries, e.g. *auto loans*, *home loans*, or high-value, unsecured *credit cards/credit lines*.

On your myFICO.com credit report you can find these listed as your Auto Scores, Mortgage Scores, and Bankcard Scores.

As the description implies, a "weighted" score relies on certain data points more *heavily* when calculating the score. For example, your FICO® Auto Scores place more value on how you paid your previous auto loans than any other criteria. Consequently, your Auto Score will be higher if you managed your previous auto loans well, and it will be lower if you didn't.

These weighted scores are the ACTUAL and REAL scores that Lenders use to make lending decisions in their respective industries. For this reason, we call them "Lender-facing" scores.

The illustration below indicates the breakdown of the "weighted" score versions FICO® has developed for Lenders.

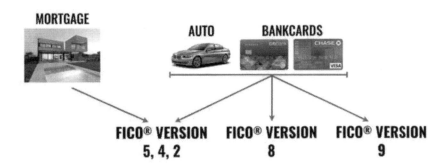

- FICO® Mortgage Scores are available only in FICO® 5-4-2.
  The score range is between approximately: 300-850[42]

- FICO® Auto Scores are available in FICO® v 5-4-2, 8, 9.
  The score range is between: 250-900[43]

- FICO® Bankcard Scores are available in FICO® v. 5-4-2, 8, 9.
  The score range is between: 250-900.

FICO® "Unweighted" Scoring Models

An "unweighted" score is VERY different than its weighted cousin. It scores the "raw" FICO® 40 Borrower Behaviors data without giving more weight or value to a particular set of data points.

FICO® offers three unweighted scores—Versions 8, 9, and 10.[44]

---

[42] The scoring range between Mortgages Scores vary subtly by Credit Bureau because FICO® 5-4-2 algorithms are specific to Each Bureau. I have generalized here so we don't get lost in the proverbial weeds.

[43] There is an additional 100 range points used to determine these scores. For example, an 810 mortgage score is better than an 810 auto score because of the range difference.

[44] As of this printing, Versions 8 and 9 are available on myFICO.com. Version 10 is anticipated to be available there soon.

FICO® Score 8 is the unweighted scoring software most used by Lenders.

In fact, they have trademarked the phrase, "The score lenders use."

But let's look at what FICO® means when they say that. Unweighted scores are used by Lenders for very different purposes than their weighted counterparts. Some of these uses include:

1. Low-value account approvals and reviews.

Merchants, retail stores, finance companies, sub-prime Lenders, and other low-value consumer accounts[45] use unweighted scores to approve new applications. Then, after you have been approved, they will use this software to review your account performance.

2. High-Value account review

On the other hand, if a Lender uses a weighted score to *approve* high-value tradelines like auto loans, home loans, or national bankcards, that same Lender will typically use the unweighted version when doing a soft inquiry to *review* your account for credit limit increases, etc.

3. Customer goodwill

FICO® offers Lenders a program called FICO® Score Open Access which allows Lenders to share with a customer the scores the Lender uses in managing or reviewing an account (see #2).

FICO® markets the Open Access service to Lenders as an "opportunity to generate goodwill" with their customers.

While it is no secret that I have a crush on FICO®, offering unweighted scores to Lenders for the purpose of creating goodwill with Borrowers does not address the Borrower's lack of education in how to judge the value of these unweighted scores.[46]

---

[45] We will be doing a deep dive into how different credit accounts contribute to the quality and fundability of your Profile.

[46] Without the education you are receiving here, you might look at a FICO® "goodwill" score and believe it represents the FICO® Score that will be used to approve your application because it bears the FICO® logo.

How Lenders Use FICO® Unweighted "Open Access" Scores

For over 25 years, I have had the privilege of speaking at real estate investment and business conferences around the country.

My presentations have a habit of shaking people out of their funding comfort zone. Some participants express frustration—and even anger—that they have been playing this Game in the dark—and without a real scoreboard.

And their frustration is valid.

And it doesn't help that FICO® has numerous REAL scoreboards.

I get asked all the time...

"How legitimate are the "FICO®" scores I get from my Lenders?"

I will give you the same checklist I give my audience members:

• *Is it a FICO® Score (does it have the registered FICO® trademark)?*

• *What version of the FICO® Score are they giving you? An unweighted version or an industry-specific version?*

• *Which Credit Bureau data is being scored?*

Let's take a moment to review an example of how Lenders seek to create customer goodwill and "distract" Borrowers at the same time.

The illustration here shows a typical "View your FICO® Score" notice offered by credit card issuers to their customers.

The FICO® branded credit score of 680 looks official and credible. But in the circled paragraph, you will see the disclaimers in the fine print.

Before picking up this book, you may have never read the fine print associated with the "free" scores offered by your credit card issuer. It is highly revealing.

Let's take a look.

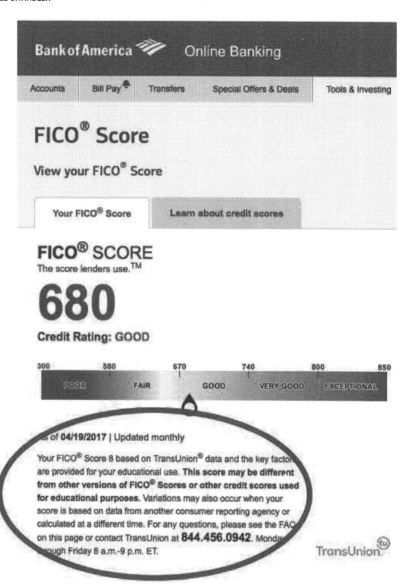

1. This score uses TransUnion® data and FICO® 8 software

The first thing Lenders have to "disclose" is also the most important. As you will discover shortly, the Credit Bureau data and software version being used dictates the score's value to the Lender AND the Borrower. We know that this score represents the unweighted score known as FICO® Score 8, because industry-specific scores include the industry type in the name, e.g. FICO® Auto Score 8 or FICO® Bankcard Score 9.

2. This score is provided for educational purposes

Because it is an unweighted score, many Lenders do not use this score to make lending decisions—especially for auto loans, home loans, and bankcards. Since this unweighted score is NOT used for ALL lending decisions, the "educational use" disclaimer is inserted to protect the Lender from liability in case a Borrower misinterprets that *this* score is what is being used in lending decisions.

3. Different from other FICO® scores

This disclaimer implies that other FICO® scores may be used when it comes time to make an actual lending decisions—including using different Bureau data and a different scoring version.

4. Different from other "educational" scores

The very words they use draw a distinction between a score developed by FICO® versus other "educational" (read: Fake-O™) scores.

5. Different from scores based on data from other Credit Bureaus

The score in this example uses TransUnion® data. But when it is time for a lending decision, the score used may be based on data generated from a different Credit Bureau completely.

6. Different from scores calculated at a different time

Earlier you learned that scores are calculated in "real-time" at the moment a Lender submits an inquiry. That is why they put the "as of..." date below the score.

"Insider" Confirmation

Over two years ago, I met a senior banking officer from Wells Fargo at one of the conferences where I spoke.

He was fascinated by our *Fundability Optimization*™ tech and wanted to have me train the loan officers in his district so they could make their loan customers more fundable and get them approved for Wells Fargo lending products.

Brad and I had several meetings with this gentleman where we got to explore the underwriting policies of this Tier 1 Lender.

In one of our discussions, he confirmed that Wells Fargo regularly sent marketing materials and bank statements to customers offering access to the unweighted FICO® Score 8, but when a customer would submit a credit card application, the bank would pull a FICO® Bankcard Score 3![47]

Not only were Wells Fargo's credit card lending decisions based on weighted bankcard scores, they used an ancient version of the scoring software.[48]

Pretty fascinating stuff, right? Disturbing? Frustrating?

Keep reading. Now it's time to learn how to use this information to protect yourself from unscrupulous big-ticket sales and financing guys.

In other words—you will never buy a car the same way again.

---

[47] FICO® Bankcard Score 3 uses Experian® data only. It is still included on myFICO.com but is described on the website as "low Lender usage."

[48] As Brad likes to say, "Older scores are dumber." This is true because the predictive capabilities of earlier score models are based on less data and more primitive tech and are therefore less predictive.

Chapter 8

Stop Pesky Sales Guys From Getting In Your Wallet

One of my most significant self-discoveries was that I was a "code-breaker." I realized that for decades I had found it easy—even second nature—for me to connect what seemed to be "random" dots, and to find the shortcuts that make complex things easier, faster, and more understandable. The funny thing was, I wasn't even aware that I was doing it. I didn't have a clue. It was effortless for me to see patterns, read between the lines, and peer through the blinds of the status quo—and I discovered I was a disrupter unwilling to accept the status quo as the final truth.

I also discovered that I had been expressing this gift for decades in my spiritual life, my family life, and in my business life. I also realized that challenging an idea, or process, or belief system was no fun unless I could share what I learned with others...

Big-Ticket Sales That Profit From Your Ignorance

Congratulations! Being an "insider" is definitely next-level stuff. Now it's time to discover just how auto dealers and other big-ticket sales organizations have been using what you just learned AGAINST YOU.[49]

Has an auto dealership pulled your credit to help you get financing?

Have you ever wondered why they pull it so many times?

It is not uncommon for a dealership to pull your credit 7-11 times for ONE auto purchase— even when you have a good/great credit score.

There is a wicked-evil reason they do so.

And it is likely costing you thousands of dollars per loan.

This is how it works...

---

[49] That is why these are called insider secrets—because everyone knows about them except Borrowers.

You see, auto dealers strategically establish relationships with Lenders that will play this Game with them.

And both Lender and dealer will line their pockets with YOUR money.[50]

They select Lenders specifically for the Credit Bureau they typically pull, and which version of FICO® software they use.

Using the illustration below, you will see there are nine different Bureau/Version combinations.

An auto dealer could send your file up to nine different Lenders to find your lowest possible score.

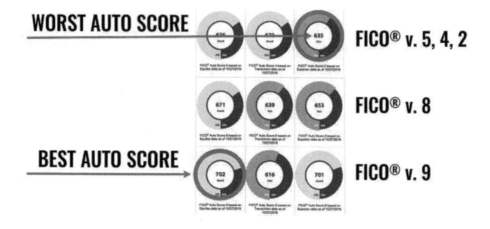

When your credit report and scores come back, the dealer will excitedly reveal that you were approved, but they won't tell you that the approval was by the Lender who pulled the lowest of the scores.[51]

The auto dealer can make money from this transaction in two ways:

- The Lender will pay the dealer a finder's fee for bringing the loan to them (the lower the score the higher the finder's fee)

---

[50] Playing the "spread" is not exclusive to auto dealers. This is a popular strategy among retailers of most big-ticket purchases: home loans, RVs, motorcycles, and aircraft. Even furniture stores play this Game.

[51] And since you don't even know what to ask, you gratefully (or suspiciously) accept the offer.

- The dealer may also make money on the *finance reserve.*

This misleading term simply means that a dealer can review the original interest rate offered to the Borrower by the Lender (the buy rate) and then ask the Lender to add a premium of 1-5% to the interest rate (sell rate). The dealer then pockets the difference each month as the Borrower makes each payment (the premium).

Your auto dealer knows how the Funding Game is played—and has been using this strategy against you for decades.

Because until now, how were you supposed to know what is going on?

When the dealer waves the "low score" loan approval in their face, most Borrowers will accept the terms offered because they don't know any different—most of us are just happy we got approved.

This devious practice can even happen to Borrowers who have good/great scores.

All the dealer has to do is shop the Borrower's credit report to his assortment of Lenders and choose the lowest score—even if the lowest score is in the 700s while the Borrower's other scores are in the 800s.

Dealers will do their best to offer you the rate and term that reflects your *lowest* score—and represents the *highest* profits to them.

Now to clarify, I'm not saying that the sales *people* are bad. I'm saying that they are playing the Game...like Pros. What you are learning here will allow you to "up your game" so you can too.

I had the opportunity of having the manager of an auto dealership in my Bootcamp recently. He was a personable and friendly guy, but I also knew he would play the Game to the best of his ability if I were to walk into his dealership to buy a car.

Even best friends will face-off as Professionals when they meet on the court.

Evidence You Are Not A Professional Borrower

Getting "shopped" to Lenders and then paying too much for a loan is only one cost of NOT knowing the rules of the Funding Game.

Big-ticket retailers can ruin your fundability by misleading you to believe that pulling multiple inquiries is no big deal and "won't hurt your credit."

You have likely heard someone (probably a car dealer) talk about how FICO® will take all "like-kind" inquiries pulled within a 30-day period and *count it only once* against your score.

This scoring policy is actually called "de-duping" and is far more complex than most Borrowers realize, and it should definitely not be used as a rationale for justifying inquiries.

In the example above, all nine inquiries may be "de-duped" and be combined into one inquiry. This "one" inquiry will count against you score for only 12 months.

The real problem is that EVERY ONE OF THESE INQUIRIES will count *individually against your fundability for 24 months* (more on this in a moment).

There are numerous ways you can foul out of the Funding Game...

And too many inquiries is one of them.

Allowing an auto dealer to pull multiple inquiries for a single loan does not represent optimized Borrower Behavior, and underwriting software is designed to find this "consumer" behavior and count it against you.

Strategies For Taking Down An Auto Loan Like A Pro

There are a couple fundability-enhancing strategies that you can use to implement this newfound knowledge and save yourself gobs of time and money—AND add to (rather than detract from) your Professional Borrower status.

Understanding and implementing these strategies will result in qualifying for the best rates, fees, and terms possible for your next big-ticket purchase.

Find Lenders With The Right Bureau/Version Combination

The first strategy is to find a Lender that uses the Credit Bureau data and FICO® Score version (*Bureau/Version*) that represents your best score.

In the previous illustration, the best score was based on Equifax® data and the FICO® Auto Score 9 software version.[52]

How do you find the Lender that will pull your highest score?

Ask Your Current Lenders

First, contact your *current Lenders* to see if they use the Bureau/ Version that represents your best score.

1. Call your branch and ask a loan officer which Credit Bureau data they pull and which version of FICO® software they use to approve the loan.

2. Evaluate the loan officer's answer using the following criteria:

   Does their Bureau/Version match your best (highest) score?

   Is their Bureau/Version close enough to what you need?[53]

The perfect example of implementing this strategy happened with Hannah. It is standard practice for all team members to optimize their personal fundability. Part of Hannah's Borrower Optimization Plan was to get an auto loan to fulfill the "credit mix" criteria suggested by FICO® scoring metrics (more on this later).

---

[52] As in this case, it is possible that the newest software version does not reflect your highest possible score.

[53] If the Bureau/Version used by one of your current Lenders is close to your best score or falls within the same funding tier as your best score, it may be OK to use that Lender (more on this in the next chapter).

We reviewed her myFICO.com credit report looking for her best auto score and found it to be Experian®/Auto Score 8. We went to her credit union to see if they would be a match.

When we arrived, credit report in hand, we were seated with a loan officer who introduced herself as Jennifer and asked how she could help. Hannah asked Jennifer which *Credit Bureau* the credit union typically pulled for auto loans.

Jennifer indicated that they pulled only Equifax® (not Hannah's best score). Not missing a beat, Hannah then asked which *version* of FICO® Auto Score software they used.

This question stumped Jennifer.

She had no idea what Hannah was asking (most loan officers don't). I stepped in and asked if it was possible to get someone from the underwriting department on the phone.

Jennifer picked up the phone, dialed a number, and posed the same question to the underwriter who answered the phone. After a few nods and a few "uh-huhs," Jennifer hung up the phone.

What happened next could not have been more revealing.

Jennifer took the computer monitor in her hands and turned it to face us. She pointed to the top left corner of the screen where we saw "EQ5" written plain as day.[54]

> *"This says we use Equifax® version 5 FICO® software,"* she said. *"I never knew that before...looks like I learned something new today."*[55]

While I have vetted innumerable Lenders to determine which software they used, this was the first time I got to see with my own

---

[54] EQ5 was computer speak for Equifax® FICO® Auto version 5—the "5" represented in version "5-4-2."

[55] This example perfectly illustrates what I revealed earlier—that many financial institutions have not upgraded to the most recent version of FICO® scoring software. This credit union was using 5-4-2 which was initially released in 1991. FICO® 8 was released in 2009—nearly 20 years later.

eyes how the Bureau/Version information was indicated on the credit union computer.

But our mission was not yet complete.

We excused ourselves from Jennifer's desk and privately reviewed Hannah's credit report. While her best auto credit score was Experian®/Auto Score 8, Hannah discovered her Equifax®/Auto Score 5 was only 8 points less AND within the same funding tier as her best score (you'll discover your funding tiers in the next chapter...).

Hannah's prior relationship with this credit union had been excellent because she had faithfully repaid two previous auto loans with them.

Armed with this intel, Hannah decided that it made the most sense to finance her new auto loan with this Lender.

Mission accomplished.

With what you are reading here, you now have one more way to make the best possible funding decisions for the rest of your life.

This is the power of knowing the rules of the Funding Game.

The knowledge nuggets you have gained in this chapter alone are worth hundreds if not thousands of dollars in interest and fee savings for EVERY auto loan you get for the rest of your life.

Make Your Dealer Do All The Work!

Another strategy that demonstrates your knowledge of how to play the Funding Game was illustrated recently by my partner Brad.

His oldest daughter was looking for a car, and in his research, Brad found the one she wanted online at a Minnesota dealership (he lives in Salt Lake City). The plan was to fly to Minnesota to pick up the car and drive it back to Salt Lake City...if the dealer could meet his financing requirements.

Because of the short timeline to pull this off and the hassle of getting an auto loan from a local bank to buy a car across the country, he used his fundability expertise to make the dealer do all the heavy lifting AND get the best loan possible.

Brad reviewed his myFICO.com credit report to determine his best *Bureau/Version* scores. His Experian® scores were the highest across all software versions and were all within 5 points of each other (*Version Score Optimization*™) AND within the same funding tier.

Calling the auto dealer, he said, *"We want this car. If you have a Lender that pulls from Experian® ONLY, then we will pick up the car this Friday."*

The dealer pulled Experian® and Brad was approved on-the-spot at an exceptional rate (even with his daughter as a co-signer).

Applied Knowledge Is A Superpower

This strategy can be implemented with local dealerships as well, but YOU must know what you are asking for and what you require from the dealership.

Are you getting this?

Amazing, right?

Once again, this one strategy alone is worth 100x what you paid for this book. THIS is another example of how to play this Game and WIN.

But we are only getting started.

Now let's explore how Lenders determine limit approvals, and how you can significantly increase that amount!

Chapter 9
When Lender "Risk" Is Not Risky

I spent 14 months in the Salt Lake County jail before I was moved to the Federal Prison System to complete the last 28 months of my custody. It was the most restrictive period of my 42-month sentence—and it was also my most creative. In my lockdown, I learned a powerful principle: limitations and opportunities come in pairs.

My greatest restriction was that my incarceration allowed only limited activities. Day after day it was a struggle to fight the oppressive boredom that accompanies a long stay in detention. There are only so many letters you can write, only so many books you can read, and only so much soul searching you can do in one sitting.

Enter the perfect creative storm...

The next Lender strategy deals with how they use FICO® scores and funding tiers to maximize profits. This information is presented publicly to Borrowers in one way, but used by Lenders in a completely different manner.

To illustrate this idea, I created the *"Fundability Pyramid."*

In this example, the vertical axis represents the FICO® Score 8 range of 300-850. To keep things simple, we will use the unweighted score, but the Fundability Pyramid™ can be used with any *Bureau/Version* you wish.

Score Ranges

The base of the pyramid represents the range (difference) between your highest and lowest score.[56]

The wider the base of the pyramid, the less fundable you are.

---

[56] Advanced users of the Fundability Pyramid™ have also used it to calculate the ranges between score versions.

From consistent student and client feedback over the years, I have concluded that a range of 20 points or more between your highest and lowest score may kick your application out of automatic underwriting and into manual underwriting.[57]

The *greater* the score range, the *less* trustworthy the data being measured, resulting in more scrutiny before approving the application.

The *lesser* the range, the *more* trustworthy the data, resulting in no additional scrutiny before approving the application.

Using the Fundability Pyramid™ as an illustration, we want the most narrow base possible.[58]

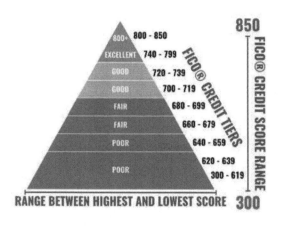

A maximum score range of up to 10 points is preferred. Many of my students and clients have even been able to achieve the *same* score across all nine Bureau/Versions.

Score Tiers

FICO® breaks down the score range into "tiers," and assigns certain values (Poor to Excellent) and risks (1-5) to each one.[59]

These tiers are ranked highest (Tier 1) to lowest (Tier 5).

---

[57] Or, in many cases, it can cause a funding denial.

[58] In my Bootcamp, students complete an analysis of their current fundability which includes score range metrics.

[59] As presented, this Fundability Pyramid™ contains more tiers than are found on FICO® and Lender documents. The tiers represented here derive from large quantities of student and client funding data.

And to add more complexity, there are different tier ranges for different industry-specific scores.

For example, a Tier 1 score for auto loans is 720+, while Tier 1 for home loans is 740+, and unsecured bank cards is 760+.

If you do not meet Tier 1 funding criteria, it doesn't mean you won't be approved—it just means that your rate, terms, and funding amount may not be the best possible.

The Pointy Tip Of The Pyramid

All FICO® scoring models have a "perfect" score—850 in the case of unweighted scores and 900 for Auto and Bankcard Scores.

A "perfect" score on the Pyramid represents the point of diminishing returns.

In other words...

Depending on where you land on the Pyramid, your Borrower Behaviors (both positive and negative) will impact your score differently.

The LOWER you are on the Pyramid, the GREATER the score change for each Borrower Behavior. The HIGHER you are on the pyramid, the LESSER the score change for each corresponding Behavior.

Let's look at an example.

Say you reduce your revolving account balances to 50%. If your score is in the low 600s before the balance pay-down, you may see a 30 point increase.

Now let's say your score is in the low 700s before the pay-down. The same exact activity may only increase your score 20 points—and only 10 points if your starting score is in the low 800s.

And now let's look at the negative side...

Say you get a new credit inquiry. Your score may drop only 5 points if you are in the 800s, but it may drop 10 points if you are in the 700s —and a full 15 points if you are in the 600s.

This is all fine and good...but how does this information help me get that new home loan, car loan, business credit line, or credit card?

Let's pull back the curtain on this Lender strategy and take a look...

Secret Profits From "Average" Borrowers

Over the last 10 years, the national average credit score has fluctuated between 700 and 710. Ironically, Lenders maximize their profits when lending to Borrowers with scores in that same 700-710 range.

That sounds suspicious, right?

Let me illustrate.

For a population of Borrowers who have a credit score between 700-710, FICO® predicts that 95% of the principal loaned out will be repaid, plus applicable interest and fees.[60]

But according to FICO® (and Lender underwriting software), a credit score of 700 to 710 would only merit Tier 2 or Tier 3 interest

---

[60] Any time I use the term "credit score" in general terms, I am implying the use of the appropriate Bureau/Version of the FICO® scoring software for each example used.

rates and fees. This means that, depending on what you're buying, a Lender could charge 30-50% higher interest rates.

Think about it—what an amazing business model! You lend to a population where you are guaranteed to get 95% of your principal back, but you get to charge much higher interest and fees.

Who doesn't want those kinds of returns with such little risk?

Flipping The Script On The FICO® Revenue Score

But this Lending model only works if these Borrowers are led to believe they are a higher lending risk. Until now, most Borrowers believe what they are told by Lenders—even if what they are told is not technically true.

But how do we use this information to our advantage?

Well, let's say you apply for a $5,000 credit card and have a credit score in that same "risky" 700-710 range.

Let's say the FICO® Revenue Score predicts that the Lender will generate $500 in revenue from you each year if they approve your application.

Here's the insider secret.

To make the same $500 in annual revenue from a Borrower with a Tier 1, 760+ credit score, the Lender must approve a higher credit limit of 2-3 times more than they would for the Borrower with a 700-710 score.

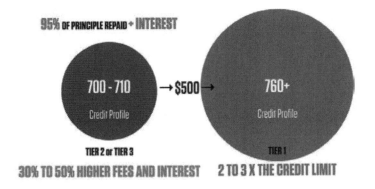

This means that with a more fundable Profile and score, the automatic underwriting software would give you a limit of $10,000-15,000 instead of $5,000—simply to maintain its revenue projections.

This knowledge, if understood and applied to Lender funding guidelines, cannot help but create significant improvements in the amounts and frequency of your funding approvals.

In the example above, you saw how Lenders label a Borrower as "risky" so they can improve their profits. But this same Lender strategy also reveals a way for you to increase your approval amounts! And you will see this pattern over and over as you continue to read.

What initially appears as a Lender protection strategy also reveals a corresponding "insider" Borrower funding strategy.

So let's keep moving—there is SO MUCH MORE to discover!

Chapter 10
Weaponize Your Automatic Funding Approvals

My cellmate at the time, Jesse, was a novice illustrator who showed me how to use the stubby "golf pencils" we were issued AND the 8' x 10' wall of our cell as the ultimate creative canvas. With the press of a pencil and the wipe of a wet paper towel, we could draw anything imaginable. This included lists (top 100 most beautiful women in the world), artistic renderings, etc. Little did I realize at the time that on this very wall, I would soon crack the code to the greatest insider secret of my professional life...

Underwriting.

It's a fancy term for the process Lenders use to decide if they will lend you money.

No matter how large or small the amount, Lenders use this process.

These approval guidelines (underwriting guidelines) are the secret sauce of ALL Lenders, and are zealously guarded—especially from Borrowers.

Let's take a closer look at how underwriting works.[61]

Say you need 20 points to be approved for a loan. And in this example, you need a minimum of three points from each of the following categories: employment history, employment length, total debt load, down payment, debt-to-income ratio, and Profile and score.

As long as you meet these minimums, a Lender cares only that you hit the 20 points necessary for approval. And they don't care how you get there:

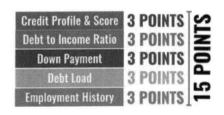

---

[61] Each Lender has its own specific criteria for this process.

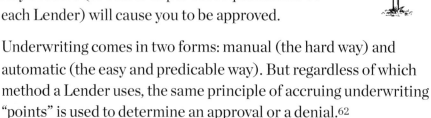

- *More down payment, or*

- *Lower debt-to-income ratio, or*

- *Lower debt load, or*

- *Longer employment history, or*

- *Higher quality of your Borrower Profile and score.*

Any of those (or others as per the requirements of each Lender) will cause you to be approved.

Underwriting comes in two forms: manual (the hard way) and automatic (the easy and predicable way). But regardless of which method a Lender uses, the same principle of accruing underwriting "points" is used to determine an approval or a denial.[62]

Manual Underwriting: The 500-Year Old Tradition

For over 500 years, all underwriting was done manually. It required a human being to:

- Physically review an application

- Manually verify the data listed in the application

- Review the proof documents[63]

- Pull a credit report

- Compare the Borrower's underwriting score against the Lender's approval guidelines

- Approve or deny the application

---

[62] Underwriting "points" should not be confused with credit score points. In fact, the quality of your Borrower Profile and your credit score are only two of the many decisioning factors Lenders use.

[63] Proof documents are the documents that verify the information listed on the application: income verification, tax returns, financials, employment verification, etc.

Because this entire process had to be done by a human being, it was prone to error, discrimination, and human fallibility.

The perfect example of manual underwriting is a home loan. Even today, every step mentioned above is still performed by human beings.

But why do Lenders need all this documentation and verification?

Because they don't trust you—or what you put on your application.[64]

Consequently, manual underwriting was designed to find out EVERYTHING about you—and obtain "3rd party" proof documents for ALL OF IT!

Also required for manual underwriting is documentation for:

- *Past payment performance (as recorded on your credit report)*

- *Debt load (how much debt you can carry without jeopardizing your payments to Lenders)*

- *Debt-to-income ratio (what percentage of your monthly income is used for making debt payments)*

- *How much you have in savings, checking, retirement accounts, etc. (so they know where where your liquid assets are so they can tap it to get their money back)*

- *What hard assets you have, such as cars and homes (so they can liquidate them to get their money back)*

Not long ago, many applications even asked you to put a value on any valuable personal possessions, e.g. jewelry, furniture, furs, computers, etc. It was very invasive from the Borrower's perspective.

And very expensive for the Lenders.

At FICO World[2018], one of the seminars I attended was about the cost of manual underwriting. A Vice President of SunTrust Bank

---

[64] The greatest source of Lender loss is from the approval of fraudulent applications.

disclosed that to BREAK EVEN on a manually underwritten loan, the loan had to be at least $38,000, for a term of at least three years, and the interest rate had to be at least prime + 4%.

The cold, hard fact was that her organization lost money on EVERY loan that didn't meet those terms.

She also shared that SunTrust could not compete against organizations that were using automatic underwriting software.

This brings us to...

The Rise Of Automatic Underwriting

There were three significant market conditions which gave rise to automatic underwriting:

• Lenders were losing billions to fraud

• Lenders were losing loan opportunities because it was not profitable to approve lower loan amounts

• Borrowers were becoming less and less interested in applying for loans because it was an anxiety-inducing hassle

These conditions created a perfect storm of Lender *and* Borrower discontent.

But what to do about it?

When I attended FICO World[2016], one of the people we met with was FICO®'s liaison with Lender underwriter teams. It was her job to help Lenders develop and implement automatic underwriting systems (AUS).

I didn't fully understand why she was in attendance until I started asking our 100 questions.

We discovered that many of the answers to our questions had more to do with Lender AUS than with FICO®'s *performance data* scoring algorithms.

It was then that I realized the FICO® scoring models and Lender underwriting systems were more intricately connected than I had previously imagined.

By the end of our week with FICO®, I realized their vision was a world free of manual underwriting and that ALL funding approvals would be automatic—simple, inexpensive, fast, secure, and HIGHLY predictive.

In fact, in his keynote presentation at FICO World²⁰¹⁹, CEO Will Lansing predicted that manual underwriting would decrease by at least 20% every five years for the foreseeable future.

Say "Goodbye" to manual underwriting and "Hello" to higher and more predictive approval amounts for Borrowers!

More Data!

Rather than rely on all the expensive and time-consuming "proof" documentation required by manual underwriting, FICO® and Lenders have been feverishly developing and testing automatic underwriting systems (AUS).

These AUS are designed to analyze Borrower Behavior data points —both historically and in real-time.

This allows Lenders to make near-instantaneous and highly predictive lending decisions.

The entire focus of FICO World²⁰¹⁹ was how Lenders could use Borrower Behavior data AND artificial intelligence (AI) to create an even more trustable approval process.

And with the introduction of FICO® 10, Lender approvals rely on automatic underwriting data and processes more than ever.

In fact, FICO® 10 promises to reduce Borrower defaults by an additional 9-17% over current scoring versions.

Approved In 30 Seconds

You've probably experienced the result of this technology firsthand —and didn't even know it.

Have you applied for a credit card or auto loan recently and been approved in under two minutes? In less than 30 seconds?

THAT is *automatic underwriting* at work.

What you may not realize is that Lenders have such confidence in their underwriting software that they have programmed the AUS to approve *higher dollar amounts* and *lower interest rates* compared to manual underwriting approvals.

Fraud Prevention

Not only do Lenders trust AUS lending decisions more, but they can also detect fraudulent applications with significantly higher accuracy.

The data available to FICO® and Lenders is vast. With the implementation of data collection and analysis systems like FICO®'s Falcon® Platform[65] and Early Warning Services,[66] Lenders have

significantly reduced their losses due to fraud—to the tune of $3 billion+ in savings each year for the last five years.

---

[65] A system that collects and analyzes the funding requests submitted by Borrowers to any of 9,000 consortium Lenders to determine variations on applications and indications of fraud.

[66] A system that monitors and analyzes every transaction into and out of a Borrower's accounts.

The bottom line is that the implementation of AUS is a HUGE WIN for Lenders.

But what does all this techno-babble mean for you?

How is this a win for you?

The Game-Changing Moment For Borrowers

To put this into perspective, manual underwriting requires you to present to the Lender numerous documents verifying the data on your application.

As we have seen, that process is expensive and tedious to the Lenders and it's a pain in the hindquarters to YOU—a lose/lose.

Since the development of *automatic* underwriting systems that do not require documentation to make a lending decision, the definition of being "fundable" has evolved—to your benefit.

The Power Dynamic Shifts To The Borrower

For centuries, Lenders have had ALL the power in the Lender/ Borrower relationship.

That is not true anymore.

When Lenders shifted from requiring "proof" to measuring "behavior," the funding-approval-power shifted as well.

Lenders gave their automatic underwriting systems *complete funding approval authority* if a Borrower met the approval guidelines.

So...

If YOU know the Borrower Behaviors that are being measured...

AND you know what the AUS funding approval guidelines are...

Who is really in charge of your funding approvals?

YOU ARE.

I say AGAIN...

If you know what Lenders are measuring AND change your behavior to match their approval guidelines...

You will be approved. *Every time.*[67]

What Is Being Measured

This is where the rubber meets the proverbial road. To be completely in charge of your own funding approvals, you must know the answers to these two questions...

- *What are the underwriting criteria and approval guidelines?*

- *How do you modify your Borrower Behavior and conform to those guidelines?*[68]

And then implement the answers.

Let's take a look at each of these questions in turn and explore the answers to each. There are two major data sets that automatic underwriting software measures:

Behavior

FICO® measures approximately 40 behaviors. Then, Lenders add *THEIR* internal performance data to the FICO® 40 metrics (much more on this shortly...).

Time

Automatic underwriting software also measures the FICO® 40 Borrower Behaviors over the most recent 24 months. I call this the 24-Month Look-Back Period and we will explore this in great depth in a later chapter as well.

---

[67] Period. End of story. The End. Capút. El Fin.

[68] In my Get Fundable! Bootcamp, I go into great detail about how these Borrower Behaviors can increase your approvals.

How AUS Use Your Behavior To Approve You For Funding

Previously, I used the example of a "30-second" approval to demonstrate automatic underwriting. Let's dig a little deeper and illustrate how an AUS would evaluate some of your data found on your funding application AND your Borrower Profile.[69]

Say you apply for a new $5,000 personal credit card.

First, the AUS will total up all of your personal revolving account limits. *In this case, $10,000.*

Second, it will calculate the average utilization as reported to the Credit Bureaus over the last 24 months. *In this case, 36%.*[70]

Third, the AUS calculates the average balance over the last 24 months by multiplying your average utilization by your total limits. *Here, the average balance is $3,600.*

Fourth, it estimates the minimum payment on that $3,600 by multiplying it by 4%. *This results in an average minimum payment for the last 24 months at about $144.*

The calculations above use the 24-month look-back period to determine your BEHAVIORS with regards to your BALANCES over the preceding 24 months.

PERSONAL Credit Application	
Total personal revolving account limits	$10,000
Average utilization	36%
Average balance	$3,600
Average payment	$144
Requested personal credit limit	$5,000
Apply average 24 month utilization	36%
Extrapolated balance on new personal account	$1,800
Extrapolated payment on new personal account	$72
Extrapolated total of new payment	$216

If new DTI ≤ funding guidelines = CALCULATED limit is APPROVED

If new DTI > funding guidelines (slightly) = Lower limit APPROVED

If new DTI > funding guidelines (significantly) = DENIED

← NEW PAYMENT TO INCLUDE IN DTI CALCULATIONS

[69] This is an overly-simple example designed to show how AUS use behavior and time to approve a new funding request. There are at least 39 other Borrower Behaviors that would be measured at the same time.

[70] Utilization is the ratio of your balance to limits as reported monthly to the Credit Bureaus and scored by FICO® software.

Borrower Behavior Metrics = Simple Math

The next set of calculations is used to determine if a Lender will approve you for the new credit card you're requesting.

First, the AUS hypothetically applies the average utilization of 36% to the $5,000 credit card you are applying for.

This results in a new balance of $1,800.

Second, it will calculate the estimated minimum payment on the new $1,800 balance, multiplying it by the minimum payment of 4%. *This results in a new minimum payment of $72.*

Third, it adds the new payment of $72 to the old payment of $144. *This results in a total new minimum payment of $216.*

Fourth, the AUS calculates your new debt-to-income ratio (DTI) by adding this new payment to all your other debt payments and dividing that total by the income you stated on your application.

Fifth, if your DTI is *significantly less* than the guidelines, you are *automatically approved for a significantly HIGHER limit* than you requested.

In fact, Lenders tend to approve up to the amount your DTI can safely handle based on your Borrower Behaviors over the last 24 months.[71]

However, if your new DTI is *slightly less* than the Lender funding approval guidelines, you are *automatically* approved for the requested amount.

On the other hand, if your new DTI is *slightly higher* than the Lender approval guidelines, a lower limit may be approved.

And if your DTI is *significantly higher* than the guidelines, you will be denied. And ALL of this occurs in 30 seconds or less.

---

[71] This insider secret and the strategies that go with it are vital to qualifying for business loans and lines of credit.

Getting Kicked Into Manual Underwriting Hell

Most Lenders today start the funding approval process using automatic underwriting systems to evaluate your fundability.

Only if something goes WRONG are you kicked out of automatic and into manual underwriting.

So what will get you kicked into manual underwriting?

There are three main reasons—and each has numerous factors.

First, manual underwriting is the go-to when there are conflicts between the information you enter on your funding request application and the Borrower Behaviors reported by the Credit Bureaus and other verification databases.

Think about it.

Who are they going to believe more...

What you put on your application or what Lenders report on you?

They will believe the data reported by the Credit Bureaus EVERY TIME—even if the Bureau data is outdated or inaccurate.

When these application conflicts exist, the Lender cannot trust your application data, requiring the need to verify your application details manually with proof documents.

Second, you are kicked into manual underwriting if there are significant data inconsistencies between what is being reported by the three different Bureaus.[72]

The CREDIT APPROVAL Process

---

[72] Not to worry—you will learn how to correct and manage your Credit Bureau data in upcoming chapters.

Page 89

And third, because you have an un-fundable Borrower Profile. Remember, there are many reasons you may be un-fundable:

- *Too many inquiries*

- *Too high utilization*

- *Too little credit*

- *Too short of a credit history*

- *Low quality of current accounts reporting on your Profile*[73]

- *Too much available credit*

Each of these reasons will either kick you into manual underwriting or get you an immediate denial.

The 1000 Foot View

We will go into greater depth in later chapters regarding how to avoid manual underwriting, but here's what we covered so far:

- *Avoid the funding and data landmines that make you un-fundable*

- *Make sure every field on your funding application matches the corresponding data point on the Credit Bureau records*[74]

- *Make sure your Borrower Behaviors hit the Lender's funding bullseye in all FICO® 40 measurements*

Being fundable means being able to qualify for ANY loan or line of credit and use it to accomplish your personal and professional goals.

Until now, like an untapped gold mine, you have been sitting on your own funding approvals completely unaware that vast riches are within reach.

Keep pressing forward!

---

[73] For example, if your Borrower Profile consists of consumer accounts and mall store credit cards, your Profile may not have the "heft" to qualify for high-value Tier 1 and Tier 2 accounts, etc.

[74] Every. Damn. Field.

Chapter 11
Exposé: Scores Don't Get High-Value Approvals

By the time I was sentenced, I had been in the consumer credit space for almost a decade. I spent the first five years of that as a co-founder of Lexington Law and the second half in my own private credit restoration practice.

Time inside allowed me to focus on every aspect of my life. One of those priorities was my credit business. I had a great reputation among my referral partners for keeping my word to the clients they referred to me. But when it came down to it, I was doing credit repair—writing letters to the credit Bureaus hoping to delete negative items from a credit report.

As I sat in my prison cell, I KNEW I wanted MORE for the people I had dedicated my life to helping. I wanted them to be able to QUALIFY for meaningful funding approvals like cars, homes, and business credit.

NO ONE in the credit repair space was doing THAT...

I meet Borrowers all over the country who come to me completely perplexed as to why they have 800+ credit scores, and yet Lenders won't raise their credit limit or approve them for even a simple business loan or line of credit.

This situation begs the question...

> *Can you have a great score and still be un-fundable?*

Absolutely. As you discovered previously, the other Funding Game Players invest a lot of money and resources to provide us with "free" credit scores, yet they don't use those scores as the primary approval metric. In fact, the opposite is true—scores are often used to distract Borrowers from what is REALLY being measured.

From our recent discoveries, we know that credit scores do NOT equal FUNDABILITY.

> *So if credit scores do not determine a funding approval, what does?*

Let's take a look at the true indicators of fundability.

The Quality Of Your Borrower Profile

Remember that FICO® measures approximately 40 Borrower Behaviors that make up your Borrower Profile. So while I don't want to be too simplistic, those 40 Behaviors DO define the quality of your Borrower Profile.

A well designed, intentionally-built *Borrower Profile* creates fundability—not your credit report or credit score.

The right Borrower Profile eclipses ANY score.

And if you build the right Borrower Profile, the *score will follow* (as will the funding approvals!).

Here is the essence of a fundable Borrower Profile:

• *An optimized Personal Borrower Identity (PBID)*

• *An optimized Revolving Accounts Portfolio*

• *An optimized Installment Loan Portfolio*

• *Accurate and consistent tradeline reporting between Bureaus*

• *Debt-to-income ratio*

• *A Profile that fits funding guidelines in these areas:*

    - *Derogatory listings*

    - *Number of inquiries*

    - *Quality of Borrower Profile and Behaviors*

    - *Utilization (especially over the 24-month look-back period)*

    - *Available credit*

    - *Recency of new accounts*

    - *Presence of authorized users on your Profile*

Tale Of The Two Roberts

Let's explore a couple of examples where Borrowers with spectacular scores were completely un-fundable, and rejected by Lenders as a result.

Robert #1 is a perfect example of a Borrower with "awesome" (read: misleading) scores, and an un-fundable Profile.

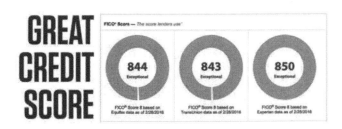

While his near-perfect scores—844 to 850 (unweighted)—would lead you to believe he could qualify for ANYTHING, the opposite was the case.

The problem was that he had a "consumer" Borrower Profile.

When we look under the hood of his Profile, this 850 score was based on one local credit union credit card with a $5,000 limit, a Lowe's *retail* credit card, a Best Buy *retail* credit card, and a Home Depot *retail* credit card.

The insider secret here is that a high credit score simply means you will likely get approved by Lenders that are in the same Institution and Instrument Tier as those you ALREADY have.

With his Profile and score, if Robert #1 were to apply for a credit card at any *mall store* or *retailer*—he would likely be approved for the highest limits and the lowest rates.[75]

---

[75] Mall store and retail credit cards count heavily AGAINST your fundability and score. More on this shortly.

Peer Lending

There is one question that is NEVER asked—until now. You never knew to ask it, because you have been programmed to focus on achieving high scores instead of focusing on becoming fundable.

Is Chase going to offer Robert (or you) a $50,000 business line of credit based on a Home Depot reputation?

Not a chance!

It will never, ever, ever, ever, ever, ever happen.

A high credit score, even 800+, simply means you will qualify for *more* accounts like you already have.

A high credit score is ONLY meaningful if it represents an optimized Borrower Profile and positive Borrower Behaviors relating to *high-value accounts.*

Otherwise, your score is relatively meaningless.

But if your Profile and Behaviors demonstrate badassery with *high-value accounts,* Lenders will get in line to approve you for more accounts just them.

In fact, the more predictable your Behaviors and Profile, the more approvals you will receive and the higher the funding amounts you will be given.[76]

---

[76] FICO® SBSS℠ LiquidCredit® Engine is designed to approve up to $1,000,000 in business credit using data from a funding application alone. Your personal and business Profiles have to be bulletproof to make this happen. I have clients who have been approved for unsecured business lines of credit exceeding $500,000 with no documentation required. Read that again: no financials, no tax returns, and no income verification. Find out more at GetFundableBootcamp.com.

Imagine $20,000 or $50,000+ approvals from multiple Business Lenders for "trophy" lines of credit.[77] Or would you prefer large commercial loans, multiple real estate loans, or other funding approvals?

Your imagination and your alignment with simple fundability principles are your ONLY limits.

The good news it that it's just math—calculations based on Behaviors *completely under your control.*

I have said it before but it cannot be overstated:

Lenders lose money when they manually underwrite a loan. They DESIGNED their AUS to save money, reduce fraud, *and increase their profits from approving higher funding amounts.*

Their AUS is DESIGNED to recognize fundable Profiles and Behaviors. It is DESIGNED to approve a Borrower for funding amounts *equal* to the software's confidence in THAT Borrower.

The higher the *confidence*, the higher the *approvals.*

Authorized Users: They Don't Live Up To The Hype

Let's look at another client who came to me because he felt he was "unjustly" denied by a Lender.

The truth was he got kicked into manual underwriting AND his credit line limit approval was reduced by 80%.

But he didn't know why.

Robert #2 had very respectable scores—780 to 793 (unweighted).

---

[77] They are the trophies of all credit instruments and getting one (or more) is proof you have mastered the Funding Game.

When he applied for a business line of credit, Wells Fargo approved him for $50,000 in automatic underwriting—with a *conditional approval*.[78]

So, when the underwriters put him through their rigorous procedures, they found that Robert #2 was actually an authorized user on his father's $50,000 Chase credit card.

They immediately reduced his "approval" from $50,000 to $10,000.

Robert #2 was pissed.

Let's do a very simple exercise to replicate the analysis the AUS performed with Robert #1's data points:[79]

• *His date of birth on the application made him 24 when he applied*

• *The Chase credit card on his Profile was 20 years old*

• *He couldn't be the owner of the account at age 4*

• *Therefore, he wasn't the owner of the account*

• *Therefore, he must be an authorized user*

• *Therefore, his approval was based ONLY on accounts he DID own*

• *Wells Fargo reduced his credit line to $10,000*

Just like you will never get approved for loans and lines of credit based on your score, you will never, ever, ever be approved for funding based on somebody else's payment reputation.

---

[78] Lender-speak for his file needing manual review (manual underwriting).

[79] This analysis is not the only valuation used to detect authorized users.

Some would argue that being an authorized user will help your score. It may help raise your score enough to get a retail card (which will harm your Profile), but even then it's an artificial prop.

Robert #2 has a high score as a result of his dad's reputation—but HE could not qualify for a $50,000 approval based on HIS metrics.

More importantly, this argument relies on assuming that a high score is beneficial on its own...

AND IT IS NOT!

Being an authorized user is completely worthless to your fundability and will actually downgrade your Profile quality. And any point increase you may get for piggy-backing on someone else's account is only worth 40% of what the owner of the account gets.

This fact was stated clearly by FICO® in our meetings with them.

But while authorized users may appear to get a small bump in their scores, they will take the same point hit *against* their score that the owner does if the account goes delinquent.

Yes, you read that correctly.

If the owner of the account is delinquent on a payment or the account goes to collection or is charged-off, the authorized user takes the FULL NEGATIVE IMPACT of the account delinquency —right alongside the owner of the account—and both Profiles will take the same corresponding hit against their scores.

THE FUNDABILITY OF BOTH WILL BE RUINED.

When I teach about this landmine in my Bootcamps, some people push back and say that this policy isn't fair.

I can't speak to its "fairness," I can only tell you it's true.

Think of it this way: The Lender doesn't know who made the charges on the account, so every user on the account will be penalized for any negative behavior related to the account.

But since the *owner* is the only party responsible for making payments to the account, ONLY the owner will get full points for any positive behavior related to the account.

Since your fundability is the direct result of the quality of your Borrower Profile and your Borrower Behaviors, I will spend the rest of this book revealing the insider secrets that will help you implement the key metrics to improve both.

Because they are so important to your approvals, let's now take a deeper look into the FICO® 40—the very Behaviors that FICO® and the Lenders are measuring.

Chapter 12

Revealed: Borrower Behaviors To Play Like A Pro

> *More importantly, my clients were not numbered among the 150 million Borrowers who had GOOD credit. Credit repair tried to help only people with bad credit. Who was out there helping Borrowers with no derogatory credit, but who were still not fundable?*
>
> *No one...*

There are two facets to the Borrower Behaviors that have so much influence over your fundability. The first are the *Behaviors* themselves, and the second is the *time* over which those Behaviors are measured.

To be truly fundable, you must first align your Borrower Behaviors with Lender approval guidelines, then maintain those Behaviors.

Let's look first at the Behaviors themselves.

The "Secret" List Of Borrower Behaviors

Let me be clear—this "secret" list is only secret to Borrowers. Lenders have had it since it was first published by FICO® decades ago. And it has grown over the years.

I have distilled this list into an ebook that reveals each one of the Borrower Behaviors that has been, is currently, or may one day be part of the FICO® scoring universe. The contents of this document are highly revealing.

To fully understand this chapter, you will need this list. Follow the link below and tell me where to email you a copy of these Borrower Behaviors:

GetFundableBehaviors.com

In official FICO® documents, these Behaviors are referred to as "Reason Codes." To quote FICO®:

"These [codes] may be used as a reference when taking adverse action or in customer service when responding to consumers' inquiries as to the reasons for declination[80]."

But there is more to it than that.

On your myFICO.com credit report, you will notice that room is provided for up to 5 reason codes[81] in each Score Version section.

These reason codes indicate which Borrower Behavior is preventing you from having a perfect score. They are listed top to bottom in the order of most to least negative impact.

The closer your scores are to 800 (unweighted and mortgage) and 850 (auto and bank card), the fewer reason codes are listed. Once you pass those respective thresholds, FICO® no longer provides any codes.[82]

So...

Pulls back curtain...

Each of these reason codes indicates a funding criterion that, if "aligned with," adds to your fundability and funding approvals.

REMEMBER! THIS IS THE GREATEST TRANSFER OF FUNDING APPROVAL POWER IN THE LAST 500+ YEARS.

Knowing the correct Behaviors to implement in response to each of these codes will ensure an increase in the frequency and amount of your funding approvals.

---

[80] Reason for a funding request being denied.

[81] Since the myFICO.com credit reports are used by Borrowers, not Lenders, the language of the codes has been simplified.

[82] I believe they do this so inquiring minds cannot deduce what it takes to have a perfect score...

Don't Get Left Behind: The Next-Gen Of FICO® Scoring Models

When you look at the list of FICO® Reason Codes,[83] you see there are 150 total codes. In our meetings with FICO®, the score developers revealed that the versions of software designed for each Credit Bureau use approximately 40± of the total codes available.

This is the reason I refer to the curated selection of 40± codes used by current versions of scoring software as the "FICO® 40."

Think of it as having 150 colors to paint with but only using 40.

More importantly, just because the current versions of scoring software do not use all 150 codes, it does NOT mean the unused codes are unimportant.

While FICO® did not confirm this, I am confident that the predictive nature of ALL 150 codes has been tested against millions of Borrower transactions, and that future versions of scoring software will use more of them.

To anticipate the inclusion of ALL 150 codes in future versions of scoring software, my *Fundability Optimization*™ process includes strategies to optimize each one.

Deeper Still

When we were at FICO World[2016], the score teams DID confirm that there is more to the use of the 40± codes than meets the eye.

They revealed that the scoring software also organizes these reason codes into 12 "scorecards." These scorecards are broken down into two categories:

• *Borrowers WITHOUT derogatory accounts*

• *Borrowers WITH derogatory accounts.*

---

[83] Note that FICO® does NOT call them Borrower Behaviors. That is MY term. But read through them and see for yourself that EVERY ONE OF THEM describes a Borrower Behavior.

More on that shortly.

For you, the challenge with not knowing the influence of these Borrower Behaviors is that you don't even know when you are doing something that is killing your fundability.

And since your OPM Behavior has been unconscious until now, you've probably been doing it for a long time.

As you discovered earlier, the longer you implement a "negative" Borrower Behavior, the more significant the damage to your fundability.

While there may be 150 Behavior metrics to ultimately incorporate into our Borrower Behaviors, we will initially focus on the 40± *currently* measured by FICO® and Lender underwriting software in order to ensure maximum fundability.

Optimizing Your Positive Accounts

When you optimize something, you make the best or most effective use of a situation, opportunity, or resource.

CREDIT REPORTING
1. Paid as agreed

CREDIT SCORING
1. Age
2. Amount
3. Accuracy
4. Look-back period
5. And many more

So what is the essence of Borrower Profile optimization?

It's to increase positive points and decrease negative drag against your fundability and score.

Here's how it works...

Let's say your positive accounts contribute between 5 and 50 points to your credit score.[84]

When it comes to an auto loan or any account that is *not* delinquent, credit *reporting* says your account is *"Current" or "Paid as Agreed."*

Until now, the *"Paid as Agreed"* status on your credit report may have been the only thing you were aware of and therefore, all you cared about.

But is it all that matters?

Not even close!

Credit *reporting* may report *Paid as Agreed,* but FICO® is looking at the age, amount, accuracy, look-back period, and 36 other characteristics.[85]

FICO® and Lender underwriting software weighs in and asks:

- *How long has the account been open?*

- *What was the original loan amount?*

- *What is your current balance?*

- *How accurate is the data being reported?*

- *What's your Behavior been over the last 24 months, etc.*

In comparison, the notation *"Paid as Agreed"* just keeps you in good standing with your CURRENT Lender.

To refer back to our NBA analogy—paying your bills on time just keeps you on the team. It doesn't put you on the court, nor give you the ball, nor does it help you score!

---

[84] This point range differs based on your scorecard and where your scores are on the Fundability Pyramid™.

[85] Be careful here. The positive indicator "Paid as Agreed" may give you a false sense of success. Behind the scenes, FICO® software may be downgrading the value of that account to your Profile based on other FICO® 40 factors.

And while *Paid as Agreed* may help you have a *good* relationship with that particular Lender, it may not help you have a GREAT relationship. It means that THIS Lender may NOT increase your limits, or lower your interest rate, or even approve you for future funding requests.

We want each Borrower Behavior to give us the MAXIMUM possible points for every positive account in our Borrower Profile.

This not only raises your score, but it also SHOUTS to every Lender —current and future—that you are a PRO Borrower and can play the Funding Game successfully to the Lender's benefit as well as your own.

Optimizing Derogatory Listings

Derogatory listings work the same way but in reverse. Let's say a derogatory listing can count 5 to 50 points *against* you.

CREDIT REPORTING
1. Unpaid

CREDIT SCORING
1. Age
2. Amount
3. Accuracy
4. Look-back period
5. And many more

While credit *reporting* indicates a collection listing as *Unpaid*, FICO® is looking at it through a much broader *scoring* lens.

Similar to positive listings, FICO® software is asking:

• *How old is it?*

• *What is the amount owed?*

- *How accurate is it reported between all three Bureaus?*

- *What's the look-back period performance over time?*

- *How long has it been since the most recent delinquency?*

There is more to this account than just the *Unpaid* reporting status. FICO® software is designed to measure how this status affects Lender confidence as well.

The Trigger Point Of Fundability Optimization™

Put simply, your goal is to *maximize* the positive points that FICO® measures for EVERY *positive* account, even if all YOU see is *Paid as Agreed* on your Borrower Profile.

But there is so much more going on behind the scenes.

At the same time, you want to *decrease* the negative drag against your Profile by optimizing your derogatory listings so they have the least negative impact.

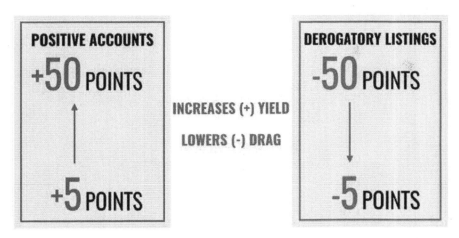

Increase positive points and *decrease* the drag against your Profile— that is the essence of optimization.

Is this making sense?

There are many ways to improve your Borrower Profile and fundability without having to delete derogatory listings.

The proof of this is in the fact that I have many fundable clients with 800+ credit scores who still have derogatory listings on their Profiles.

The endgame of *Fundability Optimization*™ is an optimized, fundable, 800+ Borrower Profile AND the Borrower Behaviors to keep it that way.

Up next...

Let's see how we can leverage time to maximize your funding approvals!

Chapter 13

The Most Powerful 24 Months Of Your Funding Life

> *That's when it came to me. If I could OPTIMIZE any Borrower Profile—good or bad—to meet FICO® and Lender approval guidelines, Borrowers could get approved for anything.*
>
> *The key was to discover what FICO® measured on a Borrower Profile by comparing client Profiles that had gotten funding approvals with Profiles that had not.*
>
> *It was GAME ON...*

So now that you've discovered the importance of the Borrower Behaviors measured by FICO® and Lenders...

It's time to learn how these same Borrower Behaviors are measured over time, and how the length of time you implement those Behaviors significantly impacts your fundability.

Throughout this book, I have referred to the 24-month look-back period[86] as an important metric used by FICO® and Lenders.

The name may not be fully descriptive because it could be interpreted that only the full 24 months is meaningful to the measurement.

That is incorrect.

Increments of the 24 months contribute significantly to this measurement as well.

The look-back period is broken down into exponential intervals of 3, 6, 12, and 24 months where the Value-Contribution of each interval is a multiple of the previous. This means you don't have to wait 24 months for a new behavior to affect your Profile and fundability—even 3 months can make a difference.

Three months is what an AUS treats as a short-term Behavior.

---

[86] I use this term to provide a simple description of a very complex metric used by FICO® and Lenders.

But short-term Behaviors are not the only thing that the 3-month period is designed to measure. It also measures financial *events*.

For example, it can account for financial shortfalls or emergencies like the temporary heavy use of credit and higher balances due to holiday or back-to-school shopping, weddings, funerals, and even a late payment. For most Borrowers, these events are short-lived and their Behaviors return to normal within the 3 month period.

Thankfully, FICO® and AUS take these events into account in their software calculations.

The good news is that Borrowers do not have to be negatively affected by these financial events in the long-term, and can rebound in the next 3-month period with more fundable Behaviors.

Alternatively, financial windfalls (selling a house, gaining an inheritance, receiving a big bonus, etc.) used to pay down all your credit card balances, pay off a car loan, or make a down payment will cause only a short-term bump in positive activity. Because these windfalls are *events*, and not long-term Behaviors, the positive effect will NOT be meaningful to your fundability after the 3-month interval.[87]

So, having accounted for short-term financial *events*, let's now look at how a positive *Behavior* is evaluated over the 3, 6, 12, and 24-month intervals.

To put this model in simple terms, each time interval predicts (roughly) that a Borrower's Behavior over a specific time period indicates that the same Behavior will be exhibited for the same period of time in the future.

Let's say you start paying off one of your credit cards to a $0 balance by the due date/time for 3 months in a row. FICO® and AUS predict

---

[87] In some circumstances, I may recommend a longer-term pay down of credit card balances instead of a lump-sum payment. If implemented correctly, this strategy transforms an "event" into a positive "behavior" and results in a significant long-term boost to fundability. WARNING: Your case may be different and this strategy could harm rather than help your situation.

you will likely continue that same Behavior for at least the *next 3 months* and, as a result, will award "**x**" points to your Profile and fundability because they can count on that Behavior to continue.

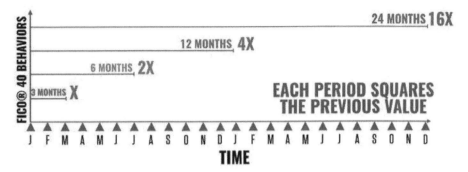

And if your $0 balance Behavior is consistent for *6 months*, the software predicts you will likely do so for at least 6 MORE months into the future.

This predictability makes you even more safe of an investment and the AUS awards your fundability **2x** more than that of the 3-month period.

If this behavior continues for *12 months*, then your Behavior is predicable for the *next 12 months* and this Behavior becomes **4x** more valuable to the Lender.

Finally, if this same Behavior is consistent for the full 24-month look-back period, the software predicts that you are a safe bet for *at least* the NEXT TWO YEARS and it awards your Profile with **16x** the initial 3-month value.

In other words, a full 24 months of a positive Behavior makes you bulletproof regarding THAT measured Behavior.

Imagine how fundable you will be after implementing ALL FICO® 40 Behaviors for 24 months.

What could you do as a Professional Borrower with all that juice?

Implementing positive Behaviors measured by FICO® and AUS over longer and longer periods of time will *guarantee* that your current Lenders will raise your limits and approve more loans.

Not only that—future Lenders will review your Profile and immediately see how little risk you represent to them, and will approve you for both personal AND business funding requests.

The opposite is also true.

If you carry too high of a balance that triggers a FICO® negative indicator for 3 months, it will have "**x**" negative effect because the software predicts that you will continue to carry that balance for another 3 months.

This is measured as "kinda risky" Behavior.

And if you carry that same balance for 6 months, 12 months, or 24 months, the software will predict that you will continue to carry that balance for the corresponding months into the future.

This is measured as "very risky" Behavior.

These predictions of continued NEGATIVE Behavior have devastating effects on your Profile and your fundability.

The #1 reason for your lack of fundability is that you haven't known what Borrower Behaviors are being measured, nor how to implement those Behaviors in a way that will guarantee more and more funding approvals.

The message here is that TIME MATTERS...A LOT.

In fact, having studied all 150 FICO® Reason Codes extensively, I can say with confidence that TIME is the MOST significant factor in calculating your fundability.

This principle is so far-reaching that every chapter hereafter will include examples of how to use the 24-month look-back period to increase your fundability.

Major Meaningful Measurements

What are some of the significant Behaviors measured in the 24 month look-back period? Without getting into the grit of a complex answer, some of the meaningful Behaviors measured with a revolving account include:

1. Age of the account

The first meaningful threshold of an account's age is 24 months. It goes up from there, but an account doesn't have much Value-Contribution until it is 24 months old.

2. Balance

How long have you been carrying a balance?

3. Utilization

What is your average utilization over the last 3, 6, 12, and 24 months?

4. Payment status

How many on-time payments[88] have you made in each measured interval?

5. Traffic consistency

How much do you charge up and pay off on this account over the various intervals?

If you are as blown away as I was the first time I learned the "truth" of what being fundable really means, and you want more information on these insanely valuable strategies...

If you want to know exactly how to be the most fundable you can possibly be...

If you want to dive into these secret topics known only to industry insiders...

---

[88] Defined as payments made by the due date/time.

I invite you to join me at my Bootcamp and learn how to implement these fundability strategies and improve *your* fundability!

In it, I am able to dive deeper into fundability—both personal and business—than these pages will allow. It also allows me to answer all the questions you may have about how every one of these strategies can be used to solve your specific funding situation.

As a reader of my book, I'd like to privately invite you to check it out. There's literally nothing else out there that compares to it.

But please don't share this link with just anybody—or show too many people—unless they are interested in what you are learning here.

Your Bootcamp experience will be so much more valuable to you if you have even some of these principles already under your belt.

Check it out:

GetFundableBootcamp.com

Chapter 14
How Lenders Created The Borrower Identity Crisis

Over the following months of uninterrupted 18-hours-per-day isolation, using my humble golf pencil and a legal pad, I outlined a revolutionary technology that I would later call Fundability Optimization™. With this completely new framework, I mentally revisited the Borrower Profiles I had worked with to remember what factors determined my clients' funding approvals. Wave after wave of awareness flooded me and I began to connect dots I never even knew could be connected...

For hundreds of years, Lenders sat face-to-face with Borrowers and physically reviewed "proof" documents that verified the Borrower's identity and ability to repay.

Today these documents include a driver's license, a social security card, pay stubs, tax returns, etc.

In manual underwriting, it matters very little what information is put on a funding application, because the very nature of manual underwriting requires the Lender to verify everything with proof documents.

Borrowers could use any version or combination of their identity. They could complete the application as Stephen Danns, or Stephen M Danns, or Stephen Michael Danns—with no impact on whether or not the application would be approved.

The Borrower AND Lender knew it would be verified with a physical driver's license.

That is NOT the case with automatic underwriting systems.

In automatic underwriting mode, Lender profits shrink significantly when a human being gets involved in the application review process.

In fact, the whole point of AUS is to leverage artificial intelligence algorithms to remove humans from the application process completely.[89]

It cannot be said enough...Lenders do not want to rely on "proof" documents. It costs too much to collect and verify them.

When was the last time you were asked for your driver's license when completing an online application?

The Great Lender Failure

More and more Lenders adopt AUS every year. The problem is that Lenders have NOT brought Borrowers up to speed with what AUS means for the funding approval process.

This is a HUGE problem.

And Lenders' greatest failure is probably the fact that Borrowers do not have a single clue as to how important their identity is to the automatic underwriting process.

Now, Lenders are spending billions of dollars every year trying to prevent the very fraud that is the natural result of their failure to educate Borrowers on the successful use of a designated Personal Borrower Identity (PBID).

By the time AUS came online, most Borrowers had already completed a multitude of applications the old-fashioned way—and used numerous versions of their identity while doing so. Since Credit Bureaus collect EVERYTHING submitted on an application, the damage was already done.

AUS had to be designed to sort through all the Borrower identity versions residing on the Credit Bureau databases, AND determine

---

[89] The use of machine learning and artificial intelligence to approve funding applications and curb fraud have been the most promoted topics at the last three FICO World conferences.

an accurate data set representing the person submitting the application.

The fact that a Borrower was approved previously for funding using any one of several name or address versions IS the "hole in the armor" that allows fraudsters to deceive Lenders into approving *fraudulent* applications in that Borrower's name.

This "hole in the armor" is a threat to all Lenders—and Borrowers.

Someone attempting to commit application fraud can do so quite easily, just by knowing ANY of the Borrower's identity variations.

For example, if applications have already been approved for Stephen Danns, or Stephen M Danns, or Stephen Michael Danns, then a fraudster could submit an application using ANY one of those names and likely be successful.

To combat this fact, billions of dollars have been spent by FICO® and Lender AUS developers to add more and more complex data point analyses to determine if an application is legitimate.

This chapter will provide you the education you should have received by Lenders. You will discover how to create and maintain a Personal Borrower Identity (PBID) that helps Lender AUS know, WITHOUT A DOUBT, that *your* applications are legit.[90] This process will also ensure the highest possible protection against having fraudulent applications submitted in your name.

---

[90] Lenders...you're welcome!

Causes Of The Borrower Identity Crisis

How did your identity become such a mess in the first place? There are many ways this could have happened. You may have:

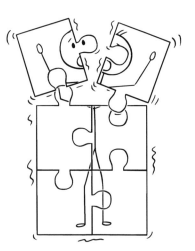

- *Used different versions of your name when you submitted funding applications over the years*

- *Used different addresses in your applications*

- *Purchased multiple homes (and each address is listed on your Borrower Profile as your "current" address)*

- *The social security number of your spouse or family member recorded on your Profile from filing joint applications*

- *Multiple dates of birth from file merges*

- *Changed your name when you got married*

- *Changed your name when you got divorced*

- *A common name and your file was merged on the Credit Bureau databases with someone sharing your name*

- *You may be a Jr. or a Sr. or I, II, or III*

The true tragedy of this Borrower identity crisis is that every cause listed above can be prevented with even a little Borrower education.

My personal story is a perfect example of the lack of this training. My dad and I share the same name, but my birth certificate does not have a "Jr." listed.

To make matters worse, I was never consistent with which version of my name I used on applications.

I filed some applications using my full middle name, while on others I used only my middle initial, and on others still, I used only my first and last name.

As I continued to research how to solve *my* Borrower identity crisis, I discovered that there were numerous versions of the name "Merrill Chandler" on Credit Bureau databases.[91]

Other Merrill Chandlers include an emergency room surgeon in Oakland, California, and a Professor Emeritus at the University of Illinois Urbana-Champaign.

This doesn't even include the dozen or so Chandler Merrills.[92]

While this represents a huge mess, there is a way to fix it.

I had to learn all of this over decades of trial and error. Thank the Funding Approval Gods that you get to cheat and do this the easy way!

The Power Of Your PBID

After seeing the funding successes of thousands of clients and students who have implemented *Fundability Optimization*™ strategies, I can say without reservation that in my experience, an intentionally-crafted Personal Borrower Identity has a powerful influence over your funding approvals AND can protect you from fraud. I define an optimized PBID as:

• *A single version of your name, address, phone number, date of birth, and social security number used when completing a funding application*

---

[91] I am NOT saying there are dozens of human beings named Merrill Chandler. This proves the very point I am making. There are dozens of data sets that include variations of the name Merrill Chandler, collected from ALL the Merrill Chandler humans on the Credit Bureau databases. AUS has to sort through ALL of them, UNLESS I provide a clear PBID when I apply.

[92] Name reversals are common in Credit Bureau identity listings and count against you as an "alias" or "AKA" (also known as).

- *The ONLY set of identity data on record with the Credit Bureaus and fraud detection databases such as FICO® Falcon® Platform, Early Warning Services®, etc.*

When you connect the dots, it makes total sense.

The fewer versions of your identity data needing to be analyzed by AUS increases the likelihood of approval because YOU can be easily identified as a legitimate Borrower.

Lender confidence goes up, fundability goes up, and your score improves as well.

If you have not already ordered your Borrower Profile from myFICO.com, do so now. It will help you as you continue through the next few chapters.

If you have ordered it, look at how many versions of your identity are listed in the *Personal Information* section.

To see an even bigger identity mess, look at your raw data Consumer Disclosure files available from each of the Credit Bureaus at AnnualCreditReport.com. You may find even MORE versions of your name, address, phone number, DOB, and SSN.[93]

Enter AUS

Let's look at this from the AUS perspective. Let's say you have five name versions and five addresses.

That means an AUS has 25 identity data sets to evaluate in order to determine the legitimacy of your identity.

Add an extra SSN or wrong DOB in the mix and AUS software has even more possible identities to sort through.

That also means millions of identity data sets can be used in fraudulent applications.

---

[93] Short for Date of Birth and Social Security Number, respectively.

Solving Your Borrower Identity Crisis

There is a solution to this Borrower identity crisis. Or better said, there are as many solutions to this crisis as there are Borrowers.

And since there is no way I can provide a custom identity solution for every reader, I think it best to outline the overarching strategies that will make the most difference for the most number of readers.

When reviewing the implementation steps below, questions will arise which require individual answers.

For specific answers to address your particular situation, I will refer you to my Bootcamp so that you can implement the steps needed to create a custom solution for *your* Personal Borrower Identity crisis.

Steps To Creating Your Personal Borrower Identity

To go any further down the path to fundability, you MUST create a fundable PBID.[94] The steps below will help you establish only ONE version of your identity reported by the Credit Bureaus—and then use ONLY that identity when completing future funding requests:

1. Order your myFICO.com credit report

The "Advanced" monitoring option on this site will give you access to your true FICO® credit scores and will help you establish a baseline as you seek to improve your fundability.

2. Order ALL three of your Consumer Disclosure Files

These are your raw data files—one each from Equifax®, TransUnion®, and Experian®.

You'll find your disclosure files at: AnnualCreditReport.com

---

[94] The intention of a PBID is to clarify your REAL identity and ensure it is the only one associated with your data set. Establishing a fundable PBID does NOT include using a Credit Protection Number (CPN) or Individual Taxpayer Identification Number (ITIN). Fraudsters use these otherwise legal identification numbers to create false Social Security numbers. To protect yourself from the fraudulent use of these numbers, check out the "Protect Your Identity" and "A Fundable Identity" podcast episodes at GetFundablePodcast.com.

These files contain the identity data you have submitted throughout your financial life, and are the source of your Borrower identity problems.[95]

3. Review ALL the identity versions that are listed on each of the files from Step 1 and Step 2 above

You will need to be familiar with these identity variations when it comes to disputing them at each respective Credit Bureau in Step 7.

4. Choose one version of your name to use in ALL financial transactions that will report to the Credit Bureaus

Since over 60% of all funding applications ask for only a middle initial, I recommend to my students and clients that they use their middle initial (if they have one).

Do not make up a middle initial if you don't have one—just use your first and last name and leave the middle name/middle initial blank.[96] Hyphenated names carry special problems.

5. Look up your residence address on the USPS.com website and determine its "Standard Format"

Every address in the United States has a "standard format" for how it is spelled, used, and listed. Credit Bureaus and Lenders use this format in their software.

Find your residence address and learn its standard format. This format will be REQUIRED when completing Step 6 and Step 8 below. Using post office boxes or commercial mailboxes (mail receiving agencies) like Mail Boxes Etc. or The UPS Store will, in most cases, trigger fraud detection "red flags" and your application may be denied.

---

[95] Warning: If any of the Credit Bureaus require proof of identification to send your disclosure file, you can be sure that your identity is so messed up that even the databases don't trust who you really are. Follow their instructions to get your reports.

[96] Jessica "Gunslinger" Tabora, my business partner and a member of my Executive Team, had a friend who told the story that when she was completing her first credit application, the application specifically asked applicants to put something in each field. Not knowing better, when asked for a middle initial in the name section, she wrote an "A" even though she had no middle name. Years later, when Jessica heard the story, her friend's identity data still included an "A" as the middle initial in her name.

6. Call each Lender that is currently reporting an OPEN and POSITIVE account to the Credit Bureaus, and update the Lender account information with your chosen PBID

DO NOT update ANY other financial information except as mentioned above. Verify that your Lender has changed the account information to reflect your PBID by calling again and asking the Lender representative to tell you what your identity data points are.

Do not stop requesting they update your file until it is PERFECT.

Verify. Verify. Verify.

7. Contact each Credit Bureau and dispute ALL other versions of your identity information

Whichever contact method you use, the Credit Bureaus will require you send them a copy of your driver's license and social security card for proof.

Note: Because of the Real ID Act, it is unlikely that your DMV will allow you to change your middle name to your middle initial on your driver's license.

Other than that, you will need to make sure the address on your driver's license reflects your chosen PBID, otherwise the Credit Bureaus will NOT update their records or delete other versions of your identity data points.

8. Complete each funding request application using your EXACT PBID data

You must complete ALL new funding applications using your EXACT PBID data points.

If you don't, you will just add a *new* version to your set of data points and all your efforts to clean up your PBID will be wasted.

9. Implement mail, phone, and online protection strategies[97]

---

[97] If you purchased the "bonus" materials as a part of ordering this book, an identity protection ebook is included. My Bootcamp shows you how to implement these identity protection strategies as well.

PBID Endgame

The purpose of this identity synchronization exercise is to transform your PBID...

FROM THIS:

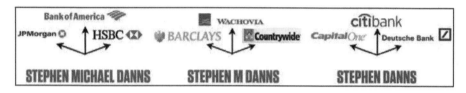

TO THIS:

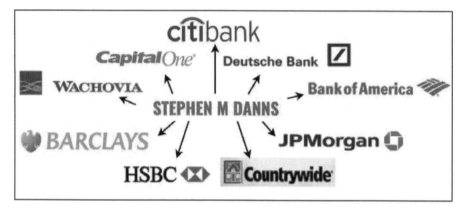

You will know you've arrived when the Credit Bureaus (and therefore ALL Lenders who pull your Borrower Profile) have access to only ONE VERSION of your identity data.

This will ensure you are not "red-flagged" by underwriting software —or worse, denied because your data isn't trustworthy and they don't want to spend the time and money to do manual underwriting.

FIX YOUR PBID NOW!

Let's keep moving...it's time to talk about how to increase the amount of every approval you get!

Chapter 15
Less Is Better Than More: Not Just A Piece Of Plastic

Probably my most significant epiphany during this period was that there was far more to funding approvals than a credit score. It finally dawned on me that it was more important to have a "fundable" Borrower Profile than it was to have a good credit score. FICO® and the Lenders have always known this, but the Funding Approval Gods weren't talking—at least to Borrowers. In fact, there was a deafening silence from Funding Mount Olympus...

READER ALERT!

I am providing these fundability principles for educational purposes only. Any loss of credit score points or fundability due to the incorrect implementation of any strategy presented here is your responsibility. Consider this actual and constructive legal notice.

Two important factors determine how your revolving accounts contribute to your fundability:

• *The type and quality of your revolving accounts*

• *Your revolving accounts Behaviors*

Understanding and implementing these measured aspects can mean the difference between qualifying for a $50,000 business line of credit and a $5,000 one.

The quality of your revolving accounts and your Behaviors related to them have a far-reaching effect on your general interest rates, the term of your "0% interest" offers, and even when a Lender will raise or lower your credit limit.

I've been referring to this chapter throughout the entire book. It's time for the big REVEAL about your revolving credit accounts. We'll explore:

• *How they impact your Borrower Profile*

• *How they contribute to your fundability*

• *What messages you send with your revolving account Behavior*

What Is A Revolving Account?

First, let's establish some definitions. A revolving account is a type of credit instrument that allows a user to make purchases now and pay for them later. There are three types of revolving accounts:

Credit card

Credit cards are the most common form of revolving credit and represent a significant contribution to the world economy.

Credit card features include:

- *Fixed credit limit*

- *An interest-free grace period of 15 to 30 days before payment is due*

- *Option for a monthly minimum payment*

- *The entire limit can be used or paid off at any time*

- *Convenience checks are sometimes issued for use with the account*[98]

Charge card

A charge card is a revolving account that requires any balance be completely paid off by the due date/time. Diners Club® and some American Express® accounts are examples of charge cards.

When evaluating a charge card on a Borrower Profile, I downgrade its contribution by 20% because several score metrics are missing, e.g. limit, utilization, optimized balances, etc.

Charge card features include:

- *NO credit limit*

- *A grace period of 15 to 30 days before payment is due*

- *The entire balance must be paid by the due date/time*[99]

---

[98] Convenience checks are not like checks associated with a credit line. Read your card holder agreement for details.

[99] For a fee (in addition to interest), many charge cards will allow a Borrower to carry a balance.

Credit line

When evaluating a credit line on a *personal* Borrower Profile, I downgrade its contribution by 20% because the availability of checks and the lower cost of interest may cause Borrowers to use the line and carry higher balances more frequently.

Credit line features include:

- *Fixed credit limit*

- *Option for a monthly minimum payment*

- *The entire limit can be used or paid off at any time*

- *Often, no grace period is available on credit lines and interest begins accruing immediately on all outstanding balances*

- *Interest is usually less than credit or charge cards*

- *Has a termination or conversion date[100]*

Individual And Portfolio Account Measurements

I call the collection of all your revolving accounts reported to your Borrower Profile a *"Revolving Account Portfolio."* This term makes it easier to refer to how FICO® measures the *whole* of your revolving accounts, rather than just the effects of your accounts individually.

FICO® counts the Value-Contribution of your revolving accounts in two ways: *individually* and as a *portfolio*.

The Message That Revolving Accounts Send To Lenders

If FICO® and Lender software are evaluating your revolving account Behaviors, then the way you treat your revolving accounts sends a vital message to current and future Lenders.

And the message you send determines your funding success. In effect, you want your message to be:

---

[100] When the term of a line of credit expires, most Lenders convert outstanding balances into an installment loan.

- *"Hey, look at all of this money I have access to (whether it's $10,000, $50,000, or $100,000) and look how responsible I am with it!"*

- *"I don't abuse it, I don't risk what you have entrusted to me."*

- *"I don't keep high balances—I engage it regularly, then I pay it off."*

- *"I treat your money with deference and respect."*

That's the message you want to send with your revolving account Behavior. And FICO® and automatic underwriting software KNOW how to interpret that message, and will reward your positive Behaviors.

Alternatively, you can send a different kind of message that is delivered and measured just as clearly:

- *"The moment I get access to a new credit card, I charge it up because I am desperate for money and I don't care about the ramifications."*

- *"I carry high balances because I needed the money and I hope that I can pay it off someday."*

- *"I make minimum payments because I cannot afford the purchases I made and I don't have a better plan to pay the balances off."*

- *"I use your funds without even a thought for how it could affect our relationship, and I am careless regarding your resources."*

Depending on the message you send with your revolving account Behavior—especially in light of the 24-month look-back period—Lenders will decide your value (and risk) to them as a partner.

A positive determination will improve your relationship with the Lender, which will allow their AUS to approve you for higher limits, lower interest rates, and new funding opportunities.

Think of it as the software saying, "This Borrower is awesome. There is little-to-no risk if I invest in them further. If they are going to behave so well with what they have already, I'm going to give them more."[101]

That's the message you want to send.

In the reverse, a negative determination will dampen or destroy your relationship with the current Lender and warn other Lenders that you will treat their funds poorly as well.

Warning! Warning! Warning!

As with everything that FICO® and Lender software measures, think of the Value-Contribution of each of your personal revolving accounts (and your entire portfolio) as a target.

While there may exist a perfect revolving *account* and a perfect *Revolving Account Portfolio,* the individual and collective quality are graded on a multitude of characteristics.

Do not be discouraged as you learn what is considered high-value or low-value and how they differ. There are insider secret strategies to improve ALL Profiles—including yours.

Fundability Optimization™ is BOTH *art* and *science,* and there are 40 factors that must be taken into account when deciding how to get from the outer rings of your fundability target to the bullseye. But great caution should be used in making ANY changes to your Profile.[102]

My point in sharing this knowledge is to give you hope that you can become more fundable.

I share it so you can see that there is a path to fulfilling your financial dreams.

---

[101] Sounds a little bit like the Parable of the Talents.

[102] If you were to learn that 5 revolving accounts may be a better portfolio size than 10...DO NOT CLOSE ANY ACCOUNTS! If you were to learn that Tier 1 credit cards are better than Tier 4, DO NOT CLOSE YOUR TIER 4 CARDS or GET NEW TIER 1s!

But beware...the path to fundability is fraught with landmines.

Please do not strike out on your own with no preparation, no map, and no access to someone who has walked this terrain hundreds of times and knows where the landmines are and how to avoid them.

Revolving Account Value-Contribution

FICO® calculates a value for each revolving account in your Revolving Account Portfolio. But our focus in this discussion is on fundability—NOT score.

From my experience analyzing innumerable Borrower Profiles, I have concluded that there are two major factors in determining how valuable a revolving account is to your *fundability*.

1. Institution Value

The type of financial *institution* that issues the revolving account has a major influence on the quality and fundability of your Borrower Profile.

2. Instrument Value

The quality of the credit *instrument* itself has a significant influence on the quality and fundability of your Borrower Profile.

From all my research while developing *Fundability Optimization*™, I found it necessary to create valuation distinctions beyond those offered by FICO® or Lenders.

These distinctions have been distilled into a matrix of 16 different values

REVOLVING ACCOUNT CONTRIBUTION

	INSTITUTION VALUE		
Tier 1	Tier 2	Tier 3	Tier 4

that help evaluate your *Revolving Account Portfolio and fundability* —but may not have much, if any, impact on your score.

In my experience, these added distinctions have yielded not only greater Borrower understanding of this principle, but have allowed me to reconcile the different priorities held by FICO® and Lenders respectively.

Because of their powerful influence, we will explore the importance of each factor so you can make intelligent choices in the future when building and optimizing your Revolving Account Portfolio.

Institution Value

There exists a wide spectrum of financial institutions that issue a variety of revolving account credit instruments.

FICO® software values some institutions over others, and rewards or penalizes your score and fundability accordingly.

For example, your Profile will display a negative indicator if it DOES NOT have a *national bankcard,* but it will also display a negative indicator if it DOES have a *consumer finance account.*

So far, FICO® has not shared with me which institutions it bonuses or penalizes under the *national bankcard* metric, so I will bring *my* research and analysis to our discussion.

Institution Fundability Factors And Tier Placement

In determining the most fundability-relevant way to assign values to *institutions,* I use what I call *"Fundability Factors."* How an institution stacks up against the following questions determines their tier placement:

- *What is the institution's relationship to FICO®?*

- *Is it a depository institution?*

- *Does it use automatic underwriting systems for personal accounts?*

- *How stringent are the underwriting criteria?*

- *What is the institution's influence footprint and accessibility to Borrowers nationwide?*

- *Does it have business credit instruments that DO NOT report to a Borrower's personal Profile?*

- *Does it use FICO®'s SBSS℠ LiquidCredit® for business lending?*

Institution Valuation By Tier

Using the Fundability Factors above, we can now explore how different lending institutions are fundability-relevant.

Tier 1 - **National Banks**

The institutions that definitely qualify under FICO®'s *national bankcard* metric AND fulfill the criteria above are Bank of America®, Citibank®, JP Morgan Chase Bank®, and Wells Fargo®.

Each of these banks score high marks on my Fundability Factors criteria for a couple important reasons:

- *They are early adopters of fraud detection, money-laundering detection, and new scoring model releases.*

- *Their commitment to loss-prevention and risk-mitigation facilitates their implementation of AUS that, in turn, facilitate Borrower fundability.*

Tier 2 - **Regional Banks, International Banks, and "Marketing" Lenders**

Institutions that qualify as Tier 2 Lenders include regional and international depository banks, as well as what I call *marketing* institutions.

Tier 2 institutions, by definition, rank lower against the Fundability Factors list than Tier 1 institutions for several reasons:

- *A regional or international bank generally has a smaller footprint, which limits Borrowers outside the footprint access to a relationship with the institution.*

- *These institutions may be slower in adopting AUS and, as a result, rely on manual underwriting.*

- *These institutions may even require a Borrower to apply at the physical branch office to open any type of account—including credit instruments.*

- *Additionally, many of these institutions report what they call "business credit instruments" on a Borrower's personal Profile.*

Examples of Tier 2 regional institutions include BB&T®, PNC Bank®, US Bank®, KeyBank®, and Capital One Bank®[103], and many others. Foreign Tier 2 institutions include HSBC®, Deutsche Bank®, Barclays Bank®, among many others.

The final category of institution that ranks in Tier 2 is the *marketing* institution—which, by definition, *markets* to Borrowers nationwide. And while technically a financial institution, they are NOT depository institutions.

Numbered among these Tier 2 marketing institutions are Discover®, American Express®, Diners Club®, Capital One 360®, among others.

Tier 3 - Savings and Loans, Credit Unions, Community Banks
These institutions have less influence and smaller footprints than their Tier 1 and Tier 2 cousins.

The Tier placement for these institutions results from not stacking up well against the Fundability Factors list. For example:

---

[103] Capital One Financial Corporation is a bank holding company which has two divisions relevant to this discussion: an online credit card division branded Capital One 360 and a brick and mortar branch division known as Capital One Bank. Credit cards issued by each division report to the Credit Bureaus under different names. The respective credit cards offered by each division differ in underwriting criteria, rates, terms, etc. When the Fundability Factors are applied, each division finds itself in Tier 2, but at different Value-Contribution levels.

- *These Lenders may offer great rates, terms, or personal customer service, but where they may have exceptional hospitality, they usually perform less favorably when it comes to funding approvals.*

- *They tend to be "last adopters" when it comes to AUS. They rely heavily on manual underwriting for most funding approvals, and are relatively slow-adopters of more advanced financial technology that would otherwise allow you to expand your funding capacity.*

If your goal is to qualify for funding approvals using AUS, then Tier 3 Lenders are less likely to help you succeed.

Tier 4 - Sub-prime, Finance Companies, and Retail Accounts

Let's look at each of the members of this Tier in turn so you can see how their credit instruments negatively affect your fundability. All three of these institution types rank very low on the Fundability Factors.

Let's look at *Sub-Prime Lenders* first:

- Having accounts with Lenders in this Tier is so detrimental to your fundability, even FICO® has a negative indicator dedicated specifically to them.[104]

- These Lenders aggressively market credit offers to Borrowers who have experienced a financial injury including the filing of bankruptcies, judgments, credit rejection by higher-tier institutions, etc.

- These institutions take advantage of the *Rat* and *Seagull* Borrower Totems—preying on the desperation of Borrowers who don't know that better options exist.

- The credit instruments offered by these institutions can trap unsuspecting Borrowers into long-term financial commitments

---

[104] The term "consumer finance account" is the negative designation given to credit instruments issued by these institutions and your score and fundability both take a hit when you have this type of account on your Profile.

that hold Borrower funds captive—funds that are important to Borrowers while they are in financial stress.

When Borrowers work with these sub-prime Lenders, what they have been led to believe is a conscientious attempt at reestablishing a healthy Borrower Profile, actually puts them deeper in the un-fundable hole.

You may recognize one or more of these sub-prime Lenders: Elan Bank®, Credit One Bank®, Synchrony Bank®, Merit Bank®, First Premier Bank®, and many, many others.

The second category of Tier 4 institutions are *Finance Companies*. There are two types of finance companies:

1. Lenders that provide revolving accounts for recreational vehicles like Honda Financial Services®, Ford Credit®, Yamaha Financial®, Toyota Financial Services®, among others

2. Lenders that provide revolving accounts to finance consumer goods such as furniture, appliances, home improvements, etc.

- The revolving accounts offered by these institutions bear the same negative *consumer finance account* indicator from FICO® as the other institutions in this tier.

- The predatory behavior of these finance companies is revealed in their strategy to put you into a *revolving account* when you purchase furniture, or a motorcycle, or a wave runner, or an ATV, or other recreational vehicle—rather than an *installment loan* which, even in the same Tier, would be better for the fundability of your Profile.[105]

---

[105] As you will discover in the installment loan chapter, loans from Tier 4 finance companies are not great for your fundability, but they are significantly better than a revolving account from the same finance company.

The last category of institutions that offer low-value and sub-prime accounts that downgrade your fundability (and your scores) are *mall and retail stores financed by other Lenders.*[106]

We will go further into the negative impact of these credit instruments in the next section, but it is essential to understand the lay of the land when it comes to how Tiers are used to create greater fundability.

Instrument Value

As with financial *institutions*, there exists a wide spectrum of credit *instruments* that can add to or detract from your fundability.

FICO® values some instruments over others, and rewards or penalizes your fundability and score as a result.

Instrument Fundability Factors And Value-Contribution

To rank the value of a *credit instrument*, I ask the following Fundability Factors questions:

- *How stringent is the underwriting criteria for this type of instrument?*

- *How many parties are affected by the status of this account?*

- *Does this reflect consumer or Professional Borrower Behavior?*

- *Which Borrower Totem is represented when applying?*

- *Was this instrument offered/acquired as a result of targeted marketing efforts by the issuer/institution?*

- *Does possession of this instrument demonstrate an understanding of how revolving accounts are evaluated by FICO® and Lender automatic underwriting software?*

---

[106] Just because a Home Depot® retail card is financed by Citibank® or American Express® DOES NOT mean that it belongs in the Bank's tier. The instrument itself is a finance company card and incurs the scoring wrath of the FICO® model.

Instrument Value By Tier

Just as there are four Tiers that rank *institutions*, there are four grades (or levels) that rank the Value-Contribution of each revolving account *instrument*.

This account contribution ranges from 100% (highest) to 40% (lowest) in 20% increments.

When I use the term *100% Value-Contribution*, it means that an account contributes 100% of the possible fundability weight and influence available to a revolving account.[107]

Since different revolving accounts have different features, it is best to explore which revolving accounts are worth 100% of the possible fundability weight and which contribute 40%.

The intermediate weights of 80% and 60% represent the *reduced* value of a revolving account to your Profile, resulting from conditions specific to each revolving account.

100% Value-Contribution

These are the features of a revolving account that contribute 100% of the possible fundability weight to your Profile and are the most desirable to ensure your fundability:

- *Credit cards*

- *Individual ownership*

- *Offered exclusively by the issuer alone (no co-branding[108])*

40% Value-Contribution

These are the types of revolving accounts that contribute 40% of the possible fundability weight to your Profile and will penalize your fundability:

---

[107] Again, the valuations are in terms of how a particular revolving account contributes to the overall fundability of your Revolving Account Portfolio, and in turn, your personal Borrower Profile.

[108] Shared responsibility by two organizations reduces the value of the instrument.

- *Check-guarantee credit lines*

- *Authorized user accounts[109]*

- *Mall store and retail cards*

If a revolving account has a forward slash "/" between the institution and the retailer designations on your Borrower Profile, it is a retail account and worth only 40% of the possible points to your Profile.

In this illustration, GEMB/JCP means that General Electric Money Bank® is financing this JC Penney® account.

Consequently, this is a consumer finance account and has a Value-Contribution to your Profile of only 40%.

Conditions That Reduce Value To Your Fundability

There are several conditions specific to revolving accounts that diminish contribution. Each of these conditions reduces the value of an account by 20%.

These penalizing conditions are cumulative:[110]

- *Co-branding*

- *Joint ownership[111]*

- *Lines of credit*

- *Charge cards*

---

[109] Authorized user accounts and check-guarantee credit lines are each valued at 40%.

[110] Regardless of the number of penalizing conditions, no account is valued at less than 40%.

[111] I downgrade joint accounts 1) because the responsibility is shared as is the "juice" for making the payment, and 2) joint revolving accounts create a mess for couples and partnerships if divorce or dissolution occur. The penalty is used on the one hand to garner greater fundability for each card holder, and on the other to prevent possible (probable) future problems.

I offer the accompanying illustration with a degree of hesitation. It is NOT a complete representation of ALL *financial institutions,* NOR is it a complete list of ALL *revolving account instruments.*

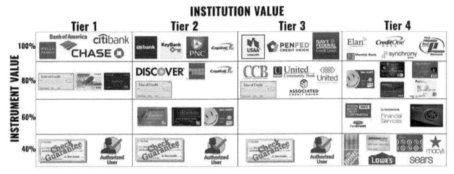

*Joint accounts deduct 20%

I provide it for the sole purpose of showing how the *relationship* between *financial institutions* and *revolving account instruments* are affected by different account conditions.

An Optimized Revolving Account Portfolio

Now that you have the basis to evaluate the contents of your Revolving Account Portfolio, it's time to explore the differences between an *ideal* Revolving Account Portfolio and an *optimized* Portfolio.

Think of an *ideal* Portfolio as the bullseye on the Revolving Account Portfolio target, and an *optimized* Portfolio as the first ring out from the center.

The *ideal* Revolving Account Portfolio contains:

- *3-5 Tier 1, open, positively-reporting credit cards—each with a 100% Value-Contribution*

- *At least $30,000 in collective revolving limits[112]*

---

[112] This is a minimum standard but may be higher depending on your personal income.

• *At least two credit cards with limits of least $10,000*[113]

• *NO closed revolving accounts*

That's it.

Because of the gross lack of education by Lenders, most Borrowers are nowhere near this ideal Portfolio and must, therefore, seek to *optimize* their Revolving Account Portfolio instead.

An *optimized* Revolving Account Portfolio contains 3-5 high-value credit cards.[114] I define a *high-value* credit card as:

• *Any Tier 1 credit card where the limit can grow to at least $10,000*

• *Any Tier 2 or Tier 3 credit card that is:*

  - *Older than 24 months, AND*

  - *Has a current credit limit of $10,000 or more, AND*

  - *Reports to all three Credit Bureaus*

If any of your accounts do not fit these optimized conditions, do not despair. Every Revolving Account Portfolio has a unique path to full optimization.[115]

Optimized Revolving Account Behavior

The makeup of your Revolving Account Portfolio is only one part of the *Fundability Optimization*™ process. While your Portfolio does contribute to your status as a Professional Borrower, your Borrower Behaviors have the greatest influence on your fundability.

---

[113] If you are optimizing your Profile for business credit, your personal limits will be based on your business funding goals.

[114] Please note that in the most recent version of FICO® scoring software, there was no downgrade in score for having more than 5 revolving accounts. But I am NOT evaluating the quality of your Profile for credit scoring purposes. These parameters are designed to make you fundable.

[115] Check out my Bootcamp to discover how to apply optimization strategies to your unique situation.

Regardless of the makeup of your Revolving Account Portfolio, you can implement important Behaviors that will enhance your fundability, as measured by FICO® and Lender software.

While there are over 40 Behaviors measured, many of them have custom implementation strategies based on your individual Profile.

Having said that, implementing the following strategies will improve your fundability and score and will NOT negatively impact your Profile:

- *Do not do "credit card stacking" on your personal Profile.*[116]

- *If an account is open, put traffic on it.*

- *Ideal traffic is 10% to 20% of the limit, paid off by the due date/time.*

- *NEVER put more traffic on than 38% of the limit per month.*

- *Unless you have been given a customized Optimization and Funding Plan, your Revolving Account Portfolio should have a minimum of $30,000 in total credit limits.*

- *Always pay the balance in full by the due date/time.*[117]

- *Always pay more than the minimum payment—even if only by a few dollars.*

- *Never make the same payment amount twice.*

- *Make sure less than 20% of the limit is reported to the Credit Bureaus.*[118]

- *Never carry a balance over 38%.*

---

[116] Credit card stacking is where unscrupulous organizations tell you they can get you "credit for your business" but in fact get you a bunch of personal credit cards and ruin your Borrower Profile in the process. Doing so can make you un-fundable.

[117] Regardless of how many other payments you make on your account throughout the month, alway leave a balance to pay on the actual due date. FICO® and Lender software measure this behavior.

[118] Check out my masterclass on reporting dates or attend my Bootcamp to discover how this insider secret will boost your fundability.

- *If you must carry a balance over 38%, NEVER, under any circumstance, allow it to exceed 90% of your limit.*[119]

- *NEVER allow your balance to exceed your limit.*

- *Keep inquiries to a minimum (no more than 2 /year/Bureau[120]).*

Up Next...The Power Of Revolving Account Aging

Another major aspect of your revolving account Behavior deals with the age of your revolving accounts and the average age of your Revolving Account Portfolio.

After utilization, the *age* of your revolving accounts is most influential.

It deserves its own chapter...

---

[119] Interest is charged at the end of your statement cycle. If you have charged 90% of the limit, then interest and fees will be added AFTER that, thereby raising your balance to over 95%. Payment of a little more than your minimum payment will drop your balance to less than 90% and you will never go over your limit.

[120] Exceptions to this rule may exist when implementing Optimization and Funding Plans.

Chapter 16
When Being Older Makes You More F*able

> *As I reflected on how powerful these tools would be to make Borrowers more fundable, I was confused as to why the other Players in the Funding Game were not shouting this knowledge from the rooftops. I reasoned that Borrowers who knew the rules of the Funding Game and conformed their behavior to hit Lender funding guidelines would be the perfect clients for Lenders—near zero-risk Borrowers. But alas, the Funding Approval Gods have their reasons—probably to protect their IP and business models...*

In the previous chapter, you discovered that the underwriting *message* revolving accounts send to Lenders via automatic underwriting software is one that indicates you have *access* to funds while using them *responsibly*.

After utilization, the *age* of each of your revolving accounts and the *average age* of your Revolving Account Portfolio are the next most valuable measurements that affect your Borrower Profile.

So it stands to reason that the LONGER you have access to funds and the LONGER you use them safely and responsibly, the MORE valuable you are to your current and future Lenders, and the MORE funds—in the form of credit limits and loans—they will extend you.

Revolving Account Aging Thresholds

The following illustration shows a generalization of the aging thresholds that FICO® and Lenders typically use when grading the age of your individual revolving accounts AND the average age of your Revolving Account Portfolio.[122]

Fundable...THE NEW F WORD!

[122] For our purposes, we will calculate average age by adding together the total months each revolving account has been open and dividing by the number of total open revolving accounts. While this calculation results in a number represented in months, it is easy to convert it to years.

As each account (and your Portfolio as a whole) passes through these age thresholds, it becomes individually and collectively more valuable to your Profile.

ACCOUNT AGE THRESHOLDS

|——————— 25 YEARS ———————|

|——————— 11 YEARS ———————|

|——————— 6 YEARS ———————|

|——————— 3 YEARS ———————|

|——————— 2 YEARS ———————|

This increased value is reflected in a higher credit score, more underwriting points, and ultimately results in a more fundable Borrower Profile.

As with many fundability metrics, aging thresholds follow a relatively exponential pattern—each subsequent threshold is near double the previous one.

The *longer* you have an account, the more *valuable* it is.

Destructive Behaviors That Ruin Your Aging Metrics

Lenders have not educated Borrowers on the importance of account and Portfolio aging. In fact, the opposite is true.

Borrowers have been incentivized by Lenders to abuse, misuse, and ruin the Golden Goose of their personal Borrower Profiles— especially with regards to aging metrics.

Typically, these incentives come at a huge cost to Borrowers while creating significant profits for Lenders.

There are four major negative Behaviors associated with account aging—promoted and reinforced by Lenders—and each harms your Borrower Profile:

- *Discounts offered for completing an account application*

- *Debt-shifting*

- *Reward-hopping*

- *Travel-hacking*

We will explore each of these fundability-destroying behaviors.

I will list under each Behavior the negative consequences unique to that Behavior, and then explore the death-dealing[123] effects common to all of them.

Ruin Your Fundability And Save 10% On Your Next Purchase

It is a common occurrence to walk up to the check-out stand at many retail or mall stores and be offered a 10-15% discount if you complete an account application.

This is NOT good.

This negative Borrower Behavior is not only destructive, but it is also EASILY measured by FICO® and Lender AUS—and your score and fundability suffer accordingly.

There is a significant **NEGATIVE IMPACT** for this Behavior.

Approval for these types of credit cards represents a Tier 4, 40% low-value account being added to your Borrower Profile. I call these credit cards *"junk cards"* because they junk up and make a mess of the Profile of a Professional Borrower.

It also screams to other Lenders, "Look at me! I'm a *consumer!*"

---

[123] Death to the value of your Revolving Account Portfolio.

If you were spending tens of thousands of dollars on back-to-school or holiday shopping, it *might* be worth it.

Otherwise...it's NOT.

Saving $10, $20, or $30 is NOT worth RUINING your fundability.

Debt-Shifting

The next example of a fundability-killing Behavior is what I call debt-shifting. Debt-shifting is used to avoid paying interest on a credit card balance.

Debt-shifting occurs when the 0% interest period is about to expire on a *current* credit card—the Borrower opens a *new* 0% credit card and uses the balance transfer feature of the new card to *move* the debt from the old credit card to the new.

The **NEGATIVE IMPACT** resulting from this Behavior is that while you may save some money on interest, the balance you are carrying is destroying the 24-month look-back period of your *utilization*.

The fundability-gutting result is far more expensive than the money you may be saving in interest.

This result is compounded by the fact that you could have saved the same money on interest without ruining your fundability by using this same strategy to obtain a 0% interest *BUSINESS* credit card, with little negative effect to your *PERSONAL* Borrower Profile.

Reward-Hopping & Travel Hacking

Lenders have made it very rewarding (literally!) for Borrowers to be seduced into opening new credit cards. These rewards come in the form of benefits like free travel, hotel stays, merchandise, and even cash-back.

Reward-hopping and travel-hacking are identical, except for the benefits you get from opening a new card. To receive your rewards, you are required to:

- *Spend a specified dollar amount within a certain time frame (usually 90 days)*

- *Keep the card open for a pre-set period (usually 1 year)*

The revenue from credit card usage, represented by the spending requirement above, is how the credit card issuer pays for the upfront rewards, miles, or other benefits.

A little-known fact is that most of these co-branded credit cards cost merchants more in processing fees than credit cards that are not co-branded.[124] Those rewards, miles, points, and rebates are not free. Your merchants pay for you to play.[125]

For many reward-hoppers and travel-hackers, once the benefits have been realized and the *open* period has passed, they will close the account and move on to the next credit card offer.

The **NEGATIVE IMPACT** of this Behavior should be apparent to you now as you become sensitized to your own fundability.

Reward-hopping and travel-hacking almost always result in the addition to your Revolving Account Portfolio of lower-value, co-branded, zero-age credit cards.

---

124 Standard merchant credit card processing fees vary based on numerous factors, but usually fall between 3% and 5%. Processing fees for many co-branded cards can reach upwards of 8% to 11% of the purchase price.

125 Be nice to them.

Negative Consequences Applicable To All New Accounts

The following are examples of negative results that occur with the addition of any new revolving account. These Borrower Behaviors have a significant negative impact on the age of your Revolving Account Portfolio and to your Profile as a whole:

New Inquiry

A new inquiry will negatively impact your credit score and fundability. Depending on where your Profile is on the Fundability Pyramid™, your Bureau/Version score where the inquiry was pulled will drop between 3 and 15 points. FICO® penalizes some inquiries more than others. For example, Tier 4 inquiries cost you significantly more points than those from other tiers.

Too much traffic too soon

New credit cards are monitored closely. If you do not follow the right new account behavior patterns, you can trigger the loss of 0% interest, or cause your credit limit to be lowered, or even cause the closure of your account. Using a new card too much too soon is a negative Borrower Behavior.

A drop in average age

The addition of any new account will drop the average age of your Revolving Account Portfolio. This negative Behavior adds another revolving account to your Portfolio (ideal is only 3-5). Since the age of the new account is "0" months, the quality of your Profile is diminished significantly because the average age of your entire Portfolio goes down.

Identifiable as a consumer

If any credit card offer requires the use of a *redemption, promotion, activation,* or ANY kind of *code,* you will be placed on a targeted list of Borrowers who are susceptible to credit offers. Being on this kind of list can downgrade your fundability.

The Negative Effect Of A Reduction In Average Age

Let's take a look at how negative Borrower Behaviors will affect the average age of your Revolving Account Portfolio.

Using the following illustration, let's say you have 4 accounts in your Revolving Account Portfolio (left column). The total age of those accounts is 12 years. So, 12 years divided by 4 accounts equals an average age of 3 years.

Now, let's say you're out shopping and you succumb to that 10% savings pitch, picking up a new Target® credit card.

The total age of all your credit cards is still 12 years, but now you have 5 cards instead of 4, and your average age is now 2.4 years (center column).

Picking up that new card caused a costly inquiry AND caused your average age to go below the 3-year threshold. As a function of Revolving Account Portfolio value, this results in a major loss to your Portfolio quality because of the average age, as well as the addition of a low-value, 40% junk card.

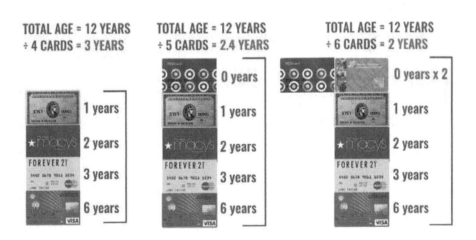

But since you are unfamiliar with the rules of fundability, let's say you succumb to the 10% savings pitch AGAIN on a trip to Home Depot®.

With the addition of the new Home Depot® card, the total age of all your credit cards is still 12 years. But now you have 6 cards instead of 5, and your average age plummets to 2 years (right column).

This Behavior dropped your average age through two age thresholds and caused a lot of damage to your fundability.

In this scenario, you would have to wait at least a full year to regain the lost credit score points—but your Revolving Account Portfolio will never regain the loss in quality due to the presence of the new low-value, Tier 4, 40% junk cards.

Behaviors Matter

Your Borrower Behaviors matter! Your messages to Lenders matter.

A lot.

It's time to stop stepping on the funding landmines and start building a fundable personal Borrower Profile that makes Lenders notice you.

And trust you.

And fund you.

Just as you learned the importance of your revolving accounts and the corresponding Behaviors that improve or destroy your fundability, in the next chapter we will explore how your installment loans affect your fundability.

Chapter 17

Stop Turning Your Back On Your Most Valuable Points

Their silence made it possible to become the evangelist of this message—a role that comes easily to me. I was committed to get out of prison and implement my game plan. I wanted to test my theories and expand my knowledge based on real-life Borrower Profiles.

Ultimately, I wanted to be able to transform ANY Borrower Profile into a FUNDABLE Profile—regardless of the starting score or initial fundability.

And the rest, as they say, is history. The results of this powerful and amazing technology speak for themselves in the lives of my readers, listeners, students, and clients across the country. I hope to count you, dear reader, among those whose lives have been positively changed by what was once the humble scribbles on a jail cell wall...

Similar to revolving accounts, two important factors determine how your installment loans contribute to your fundability:

- *The type and quality of your installment loans*

- *Your Borrower Behaviors associated with them*

Installment Loan Types

There are more installment loan types than revolving account types. They include:

- *Home loans*

- *Auto loans*

- *Recreational vehicle loans*

- *Student loans*

- *Personal loans from banks and credit unions*

- *Personal loans from "finance" companies, sub-prime Lenders, and "payday" money Lenders*[126]

What Are The Features Of An Installment Loan?

An installment loan is a credit instrument where a Borrower receives a lump sum of money to make a purchase and then pays it back over time. The main features of an installment loan are:

- *Fixed loan amount*

- *Fixed monthly payment amount*

- *Fixed term (pay-back period)*

- *You can make extra payments or pay off the loan without penalty*[127]

Individual And Portfolio Measurements

As with revolving accounts, FICO® counts the contribution of your installment loans to your fundability and score individually and collectively. I call the collection of your installment loans reported to your Borrower Profile an *"Installment Loan Portfolio"* to make it easier to refer to how FICO® measures the *whole* of your loans.

Messages Your Installment Loan Behavior Sends To Lenders

Your revolving account Behavior is about *access* to funds and how you treat them. Alternatively, your Behavior with your installment loans is a message about how you treat *lump sums* of money. Your installment loan Behavior sends the message:

---

[126] I separate bank and credit union loans from finance company and sub-prime loans because the latter are considered consumer finance accounts and trigger the same negative indicators in FICO® software as their revolving account cousins. In fact, one of the FICO® reason codes is triggered if you even get an inquiry from one of these types of Lenders. These finance companies include "fintech" Lenders like SoFi®, Kabbage®, Prosper®, among many others.

[127] Some loans require you to maintain the loan for a particular length of time before you can pay it off. If you pay these types of loans off early, you may be charged a pre-payment penalty. Check your loan agreement for details.

"Hey! You gave me all this money in one lump sum, and look at how I consistently and faithfully pay it back."

This is a very different message from the one you send with your revolving accounts, and FICO® and Lender underwriting software measures this dynamic as well.

An Optimized Installment Loan Portfolio

An *optimized* Installment Loan Portfolio creates the most fundability in the eyes of FICO® and Lenders. An optimized Installment Loan Portfolio includes:

- *At least 1 auto loan[128]*

- *At least 1 home loan[129]*

- *2-3 other Tier 1-2 installment loans including additional auto loans or home loans*

Ultimately, the perfect Installment Loan Portfolio contains these loans from Tier 1 and Tier 2 Lenders with contribution values at 100%. You do not want 80% or 40% Tier 1 or Tier 2 loans because those loan instruments are less valuable to your fundability.

Installment Loan Tiers And Value-Contribution

The framework to evaluate the quality of installment loans is identical to the one I used for revolving accounts in Chapter 15. I refer you to that section for details on how I established the criteria for *Institution Tiers* and *Instrument Values*.

---

[128] The loan can be for any amount as long as it bears the "auto loan" indicator on your Borrower Profile. The larger the loan, the easier it will be to qualify for higher loan amounts on future loans.

[129] The loan can be for any amount or any type of property as long as it bears the "real estate loan" indicator on your Borrower Profile. The larger the loan, the easier it will be to qualify for higher loan amounts on future loans.

Also, for installment loans, I use the same criteria to establish the Fundability Factors associated with the Institution Tiers and Value-Contribution for each loan.

For our purposes here, we simply need to remember that I have broken down financial institutions into Tiers 1-4 and loan contribution is broken down into 4 values ranging from 100% to 40% in 20% increments.

INSTALLMENT LOAN CONTRIBUTION

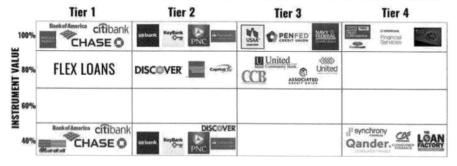

Since an *optimized* Installment Loan Portfolio contains only loans that have a Value-Contribution of 100%, you need to understand why the lesser-valued loan instruments inhibit your fundability.

"Finance" Divisions of Tier 1 and Tier 2

A significant reason for only engaging loans that provide 100% Value-Contribution is because most Tier 1 and 2 Lenders have "finance" divisions that, if you are not careful, may approve you for a loan from their "sub-prime" division.

For example, if you cannot qualify for a 100% loan at Wells Fargo®, they are likely to send your application to their sub-prime finance division—without telling you.

Valued at 40%, the corresponding reason codes for that loan will be that of a finance company loan—even if it is a loan from a Tier 1 Lender.

Before accepting any loan, be diligent in reading the loan paperwork to see if the word *"financial"* is in the title or content of the contract. The word *"financial"* is the giveaway that you are about to sign a sub-prime loan. If you sign on the dotted line, this loan will bear a *consumer finance account* negative indicator on your Borrower Profile.

And while I completely understand that you may need to engage one of these sub-prime loans in order to keep your life moving forward, I want you to at least do so *consciously.* I want you to make every funding request *consciously* and *intentionally.*

That, my friend, is all I ask of you. You are still acting like a Funding Eagle if taking a sub-prime loan is part of your overall *strategy.*

Non-Depository Lenders (Marketing Lenders)

I have downgraded installment loans from American Express®, Discover®, and Capital One® just like I did for their revolving account counterparts.

Most of these Lenders do auto or personal loans, but they carry higher interest rates and more unfavorable terms.[130]

Flex Loans

An example of a low-value loan (even though it may be offered by Tier 1-2 Lenders) is a "flex" loan. Citibank® and Wells Fargo® (among others) offer these types of loans.

---

[130] See Chapter 15 for the reason I have downgraded these "marketing" Lenders.

The feature of a flex loan is that you can choose to use the funds like a credit card OR as an installment loan.

The problem with a flex loan is that FICO® doesn't distinguish the flexibility of the loan instrument, and defaults to measuring it as a *revolving account*. If you use it as a *loan* and carry a balance as you would with any loan, FICO® will count it against your utilization metric and that "installment" balance will be measured as a long-term *revolving* balance.

This is bad.

Additionally, if you pay off your loan within 6 months, you won't get points for even engaging the loan.

Once again, without knowing the Principles of Fundability, you would step on another landmine and ruin your chances of maximizing your fundability.

Tier 3 Lenders

Interestingly enough, Tier 3 Lenders may be the only exception to the "finance division" ploy mentioned above. National credit unions, savings and loans, and local credit unions and community banks rarely have a finance division.

They usually offer higher-value instruments, and if you don't qualify, they send you to somebody else—a Tier 4 sub-prime Lender.

Tier 4 Lenders

Tier 4 is populated with finance companies, fintechs, sub-prime, and hard money Lenders. You'll find all the merchandise and retail Lenders in this Tier. Toyota Motor Credit°, Ford°, General Motors°, Honda°, and Yamaha° all offer installment loans just like they offer revolving accounts.

These are classified as Tier 4 because they lend on specific merchandise—usually the merchandise sold by their sales divisions. These are all finance companies, and their accounts bring with them the *consumer finance account* negative indicator.

Other Lenders in the finance company category are commonly known as financial technology Lenders ("fintechs") and include LendingClub®, PayPal®, Kabbage®, Prosper®, and many, many others.

Finally, the Lenders that are the "worst of the worst" among Tier 4 finance companies are the sub-prime and hard money Lenders. They include payday loans, check-advance loans, etc. and are valued at 40% contribution.

These loans are actively marketed to the Rat and Seagull Borrower Totems. Engaging these loans significantly RUINS your fundability, and screams to Tier 1-3 Lenders: "DO NOT LEND TO ME!!!"

Please avoid these loans at all costs!

Loan Value-Contribution

While the Tiers and Value-Contribution framework are the same as revolving accounts, it is very revealing to look a little deeper into how your installment loans contribute to being fundable.

Installment loans are NOT created equal.

And FICO® values different aspects of each loan.

Loan Mix (or Variety)

An *optimized* Installment Loan Portfolio has at least one home loan and at least one auto loan. These assets are secured loans, and FICO® scoring models predict that people with at least one home loan and one auto loan are least likely to default on their debts or declare bankruptcy.

This makes sense to even those of us who are not quantitative analysts. If you have a home loan and a car payment, it stands to reason that you will probably want to keep your car and stay in your house.

Having these assets makes us very aware that we have a lot to lose if we default, so we will do EVERYTHING possible to protect our financial situation. FICO® metrics have verified this fact using hundreds of millions of Borrower data sets.

This fact is so compelling that FICO® boosts Borrower scores by as much as 15 to 20 points when you have a home loan on your Profile.

And you receive ANOTHER 15-20 points if you have an auto loan.

This scoring feature is so prevalent that I receive notices from readers and podcast subscribers who complain that their score dropped 20 points when they paid off their auto or home loan.

These complaints are in line with the Ram Borrower Totem belief system that would have you thinking you should be rewarded for getting out of debt—and that your scores should go UP after paying off the house or car.

I remind them (and you) that FICO® and Lender automatic underwriting systems are the quintessence of the "what have you done for me lately" cliché.

You get points for *having* home and auto loans—NOT for *paying them off*.

Having *strategic* debt reminds Lenders every month that you are an active Player in the Funding Game.

Capsize-Proof Your Fundability

Installment loans are the ballast of your Borrower Profile.[131] Ballast is the weight in the bottom of a boat, like a sailboat, that keeps it deep in the water, so that the sailboat doesn't capsize when turning

---

[131] The term is mine. FICO® does NOT use "ballast" or "heft" to describe your Borrower Profile.

or tacking into the wind. I use this term to illustrate the positive effect your installment loans have on your Borrower Profile.

On your Profile, this ballast represents the number of positive loan payments you've had in your entire credit history.

If you have hundreds and hundreds of positive monthly loan payments, then that demonstrates to potential Lenders that you are dependable in the long term, your Borrower Profile has heft, and you are consistent in making positive payments.

The opposite is also true.

If you don't have a long history of positive installment payments, you do not look as fundable in the eyes of AUS and FICO®.

Utilization

Utilization on an installment loan is the percentage of the original loan amount remaining on your loan. An installment loan strategy that sends a great message to your Lender is making extra payments to cause the loan balance to drop faster than your loan term expires. Doing this will significantly improve your utilization metrics as measured by FICO® and your Lender.

Installment Loan Behaviors Over Time

FICO® and Lender AUS measure your installment loan Borrower Behaviors in 3, 6, 12, and 24 month intervals.

Many Borrowers like to implement a strategy to pay off their auto or other loans as quickly as possible. To account for this negative "accelerated payoff" Behavior,[132] FICO® doesn't even start adding points to your score for installment loan payments until AFTER the 6th payment.[133]

---

[132] Between the two strategies mentioned, there may appear to be a contradiction. The problem is many Borrowers pay off a new auto loan within a few months and completely sabotage the positive effects the auto loan would normally have on their fundability. This accelerated payoff is not to be confused with what I mentioned in the Utilization paragraph above. There, I was referring to paying the loan over the course of 24 months while keeping the balance above 50%.

[133] This score calculation was implied in one of the less specific answers given by the FICO® team.

Loan Thresholds

Loan thresholds represent your borrowing "comfort zone" and influence future amounts Lenders are willing to lend to you.

Generally speaking, it goes something like this: If the highest loan you've ever had is $5,000, a Lender is NOT going to give you a $50,000 business line of credit.

Your $5,000 loan amount sets a threshold—a high watermark—for how much money you've handled successfully in your previous borrowing history.

There are several strategies you can use to "raise" your threshold. For example:

- *You can engage and pay off smaller loans over a longer period*

- *You can engage and pay off higher and higher loan amounts over a shorter period*[134]

Optimized Installment Loan Behavior

The makeup of your Installment Loan Portfolio is only part of the *Fundability Optimization*™ process.

While your Portfolio contributes significantly to your status as a Professional Borrower, your Borrower Behaviors have the highest influence on your fundability.

While it is NOT a conclusive list (because I do not know the particulars of your situation), if you implement the following optimization strategies with your installment loans, you will experience a boost in your fundability AND your scores will improve.

---

[134] Again, I am not encouraging you to increase your debt load more than is comfortable for your current financial situation. There are strategies for intelligently raising your loan amounts with each additional loan so you can demonstrate that you are capable of larger and larger loans. Find out more about these strategies at my Bootcamp.

These strategies work for every Profile, and will NOT cause any negative impact:

- *Reduce any new loan balance to at least 90% as fast as you can*
- *Do NOT pay off any loan before 24 months*
- *Pay off or refinance your non-real estate loans once they reach 50% balance*
- *Set up autopay on all your loans*
- *NEVER allow one of your autopay loan payments to bounce*
- *For best results, engage loans of at least $5,000 or more*

What Really Happens With Your Extra Loan Payments

Another insider secret that we need to explore is how Lenders apply "extra" payments you make to your loan. This little-known Lender strategy is rarely discussed by loan officers.

To understand how this Lender strategy works, you must understand the two methods Lenders use to apply extra payments to your loan:

Principal-Reduction Method

This term describes the practice that when a Borrower makes an extra payment to a loan, the extra funds are applied to the *balance* of the loan.

This shortens the length of the loan (the term) AND reduces the total interest paid on the loan.

Let's explore an example of a principle-reduction method. Let's say your loan, including principal and interest, is $20,000.

Your term is 40 months, and you have a monthly payment of $500.

After Month 2, you've paid $1,000 towards the $20,000, so you've got a $19,000 balance, correct?

Let's say your Aunt Mabel gifts you $5,000 which you apply to your loan on Month 3. Now your balance is $14,000.

Using this method, after you have paid the extra amounts to the loan, the months remaining on your loan are 28 instead of 40.

In this scenario, you are *reducing* your balance AND *shortening* the term of your loan at the same time.

This method has been used since modern-day installment loans were first popularized by the financing of Model T Fords in 1913.

But this is no longer the norm.

In fact, to make a principal-reduction payment today, many Lenders make it difficult to choose that option by obscuring it on their website or making you go into a branch office.

The Lender secret I mentioned a moment ago is that Lenders would rather apply extra payments to the loan in the form of a "pre-payment."

Pre-Payment Method[135]

This term describes the now common practice that when a Borrower makes an extra payment to a loan, the Lender applies those funds to the *next monthly payment(s)*. Then, when the next payment is due, the Lender will send out a notice to the Borrower that says in effect:

PAYMENT NOT REQUIRED.

This method provides a tempting opportunity for the Borrower to not make a payment that month. However, opting for the "free" month DOES NOT reduce the term of the loan and DOES NOT reduce the total interest you will pay on the loan.

---

[135] Once again, I am using this term to distinguish the types of payment application strategies used by Lenders. To my knowledge, this term is not used in this way elsewhere because no one else is revealing these strategies to Borrowers.

In essence, Lenders advertise that you get to "miss" a payment (even though you made the payment in advance AND interest is still being charged for that "free" month).

Let's look at the results this method creates using the same numbers from earlier.

In this case, the $6,000 in payments would be applied in advance to the tune of $500 per month for the next 12 months. This results in not having to make payments for a whole year.[136]

While not making payments for a year may sound awesome, I must remind you again: this method DOES NOT reduce the term of the loan and DOES NOT reduce the total interest you will pay.

I was first introduced to this "miss-a-month" marketing strategy by the credit union where I had a car loan. They would send me a holiday "gift" each year, saying:

"Happy Holidays! Your payment this month is NOT required."

Of course, the fine print would indicate the terms:

- *My credit rating was the reason I qualified for the offer*

- *My credit rating would NOT be negatively affected*

- *Interest would still be charged for the month, but it would be added to the end of the loan*

Taking advantage of this gift from my Lender had the effect of increasing the amount of interest I would pay and lengthening the term of my loan, rather than *lowering* my interest and *shortening* my term.

However, there are certain circumstances where it is worth it to implement this method.

---

[136] Be sure to check with your Lender to determine the terms of your particular loan.

At times, the strategy can be beneficial to trigger some very powerful underwriting benefits that will build trust with your current Lender, and broadcast that you are a Professional Borrower to any Lender who looks at your Borrower Profile.

These advanced strategies require more detailed explanations than I have room for here, so check out my Bootcamp to get the customized solutions you need!

In conclusion, there are pros and cons to the implementation of each of the "extra-payment" strategies we have discussed in this section. I bring them up so that you are aware of one more way Lenders may be taking advantage of you.

Nowhere To Go...But Up

As you are well aware by now, there is so much more to optimizing your Installment Loan Portfolio than I can include here, because each Borrower's optimization path is based on specific individual Profiles.

But if you implement the strategies presented in this chapter AND this book, you will not only experience a powerful and positive change in your fundability, but you will also be able to grow more and more confident in your abilities to maximize your funding opportunities.

Take these strategies and IMPLEMENT them!

Afterword
500-Year Winning Streak: Join An All-Star Team

In December 2004, I was released from federal custody ready to implement what I had been working on for years—and ready to change the world in the process. It had been a difficult but rewarding experience.

As of the printing of this edition, we've helped our students and clients get over $103,000,000 in funding approvals while improving their standard of living and quality of life.

Now it falls to you, dear reader, to make your own determination as to the funding possibilities available to you as you implement what you will learn in these pages. Like thousands before you, I urge you on this amazing and prosperous journey.

Merrill Chandler
High-Performance Fundability Coach (and Ex-Con)

This book should have gone to print much sooner than it did. Delay after delay caused the printing date to get pushed back.

Over and over.

There were times I felt like throwing my hands in the air and shelving the whole project. I didn't know why it was so difficult to finish this damn book.

Like the Greek Demi-God Sisyphus, I felt doomed to continually push the rock of this book up the hill only to have it roll to the bottom again...and again... and again.

Then it happened...

I don't know when I am ever going to fully accept this simple lesson:

THINGS HAPPEN FOR A REASON.

Like *you* reading this book.

Or like *me* not being able to go to print until AFTER I attended FICO World[2019].

I had attended FICO World twice before and KNEW that FICO World[2019] would be awesome too. But I never thought that this new conclave with the Funding Approval Gods would have such a profound impact on me.

And on this book.

What you hold in your hand is significantly different from the original version.

Because this FICO® World...was different. In fact, very different.

A shift had occurred.

In every conversation Jessica[137] and I had with ANY FICO® team member—from further conversations with FICO® CEO Will Lansing to conversations and meetings with several FICO® V.P.'s—I experienced something I never had before.

Will Lansing, CEO

Every time I mentioned that we were committed to Borrower education and helping Borrowers become more fundable, I was met with exclamations of support:

"That is awesome."

"What can we do to help?"

"What a creative use of this technology."

---

[137] Jessica "Gunslinger" Tabora of my Executive Team attended FICO World[2019] with me and provided a significant contribution to our learnings from this event.

In EVERY conversation, EVERY senior FICO® executive I met with was intrigued by our mission to educate Borrowers—some were even enthusiastic.

BUT, in some of those conversations, several FICO® executives I met with confessed that Borrower education had not yet been a significant priority for FICO®.[138]

But needed to be.

What was different about *this* FICO World was there appeared to be an "opening" at the executive level to the *idea* of Borrower education.

This shift is evidenced by the introduction of the FICO® "*Score A Better Future*" events promoted around the country. While these events focus mostly on teaching disadvantaged consumers how to understand their FICO® credit scores (not fundability), never before has FICO® been so engaged in consumer education.

Things ARE changing...and it is exciting for me and my team to be at the pointy end of this educational spear.

"Next-Level" Borrower Education

Think about it. Why did the CEO of FICO® want me to talk to his score development teams in 2016?

Why did he give me special access to technology that is designed *for Lenders' eyes only*?

The very fact that the head of FICO® saw the value of FUNDABLE Borrowers is the REAL game-changer.

For him to introduce me to his score teams is a testament that he (and by extension, FICO®) is open to the idea that the successful

---

[138] Almost everyone I spoke with said that the myFICO.com Forum was the extent of FICO® Borrower education. They confirmed my belief that no FICO® employee contributes to the myFICO.com Forum in an official capacity. Contributors mostly share their personal experiences, but no official or formal EDUCATION occurs on that site.

partnering of Borrowers and Lenders is the next level of prosperity and profitability for both parties.

What changed when I got back from FICO World[2019] was that I saw myself even more clearly as a source of in-depth Borrower education in this country.

And the purpose of this book was made more clear to me.

So I went to work re-editing this book.

Rather than just introduce you to this awesome "tech," my motivation changed to wanting to make you feel like you had received a valuable *education—as deep of an education that I could provide in book form.*

I wanted you to feel *inspired* to do something about your situation by the time you got here... to this page.

This entire book was re-shaped to help you see the new funding opportunities that await you as you do things to transform your relationship between YOU and your Lenders.

Hopefully, now you KNOW more and can DO more towards improving your funding opportunities—and improving your LIFE.

Becoming A First-Round Draft Choice

In the Introduction of this book, you learned that the way for you to achieve your financial goals and dreams is to *build* a relationship with Lenders by becoming their *partner* rather than their adversary —to play on the SAME team in the Funding Game.

To illustrate this partnership, I'll use the NBA Draft as an analogy for the Funding Game.

Imagine you are a college basketball player. You're killing it. Your personal stats are phenomenal.

You are so good that scouts are looking to draft you to play Pro ball. They want you because of your *personal* performance. And these Pro teams want you to play for them.

Now imagine that your stats are so good that they don't just want you on their team...

They want you to be a starter...

They want you on the court...

They want you to have the ball...

Because EVERY TIME you have the ball you score...

And not just score...

You DUNK IT!

"Playing For The Pros" Will Change Your Life

Playing for a Lender is no different. When you have Pro level Borrower Behaviors, EVERY Lender on the planet will want you to play for them.

Imagine a life where Lenders can count on you for a win/win...

Imagine the payoffs *you* receive because every time you get on the court you make EVERYONE money...

Imagine the accolades from your teammates for being their clutch[139] player and winning the Funding Game...

When you make your Lending partners money and demonstrate your skills as a Professional Borrower, they will give you the funding "ball" over and over. That's when...

---

[139] The player they give the ball to when there are only a few seconds on the clock.

They will trust *you*...

They will raise *your* credit limits...

They will approve *your* loans...

They will make sure *you* have everything you need to be successful...

Because they know *they* win when *you* win...

And more importantly...

You win when *they* win.

Finally...

You NOW have invaluable information—information that, until now, has been unknown and unavailable to Borrowers.

You NOW have tools in your hands to change *your* world in every way that is important to you.

A whole new world is ready for you to explore—and new funding opportunities are at your fingertips.

If knowledge is power...implemented knowledge is a superpower.

Now...

GO make something happen...

Your future self and loved ones will thank you!

Insider Secrets
You're Just Getting Started: Time To Level Up

The most important way to ensure your fundability success is to KEEP MOVING FORWARD!

No matter how big or small your steps, you must do SOMETHING every day or every week to improve your fundability and continue growing your funding opportunities.

YOU ARE NOT DONE YET!

Below I have listed some resources that will help you to do just that. Some are free, some require an investment, but there is something for EVERYONE.

Including YOU.

Please do something. Now.

Implementation Success Resources

Check out the resources I have put together to help you succeed. Choose one or choose them all—it is up to you. I simply want you to become part of the GET FUNDABLE! tribe and add your influence to this powerful movement.

Get Fundable! Webclass

To check out a one-hour preview of my Bootcamp, go to:
GetFundableWebclass.com

Ultimate Fundability Checklist

To have me send you my Ultimate Fundability Checklist, go to:
GetFundableChecklist.com

The Get Fundable! Podcast

To stay connected with me and keep up-to-date with the awesome world of fundability, listen to my podcasts available on ALL podcast platforms, or go to:

GetFundablePodcast.com

Get Fundable! Bootcamp

Spend a weekend with me and get a firehose of advanced strategies to build fundable *Personal* AND *Business* Profiles:

GetFundableBootcamp.com

Take my Fundability Quiz

After reading this book, find out how much you know about *Fundability Optimization*™. Take my quiz at:

GetFundableQuiz.com

FICO Secret Behaviors Ebook

To have me send you the ebook containing the list of Borrower Behaviors from FICO®, go to:

GetFundableBehaviors.com

Join Our Community and Stay Informed

To keep up-to-date on this ever-changing and dynamic Lending environment, or to tell me what you think of what you learned here, go to my Facebook page:

Facebook.com/YouGetFundable

(I'd even love to have you post a selfie holding my book!)

I look forward to connecting soon. See you on the inside...